THINKING LIKE A HISTORIAN:
RETHINKING HISTORY INSTRUCTION

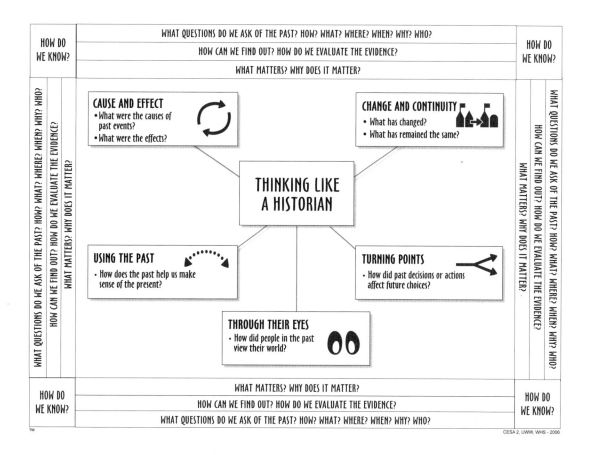

Diagram text:

HOW DO WE KNOW?

WHAT QUESTIONS DO WE ASK OF THE PAST? HOW? WHAT? WHERE? WHEN? WHY? WHO?
HOW CAN WE FIND OUT? HOW DO WE EVALUATE THE EVIDENCE?
WHAT MATTERS? WHY DOES IT MATTER?

CAUSE AND EFFECT
• What were the causes of past events?
• What were the effects?

CHANGE AND CONTINUITY
• What has changed?
• What has remained the same?

THINKING LIKE A HISTORIAN

USING THE PAST
• How does the past help us make sense of the present?

TURNING POINTS
• How did past decisions or actions affect future choices?

THROUGH THEIR EYES
• How did people in the past view their world?

WHAT MATTERS? WHY DOES IT MATTER?
HOW CAN WE FIND OUT? HOW DO WE EVALUATE THE EVIDENCE?
WHAT QUESTIONS DO WE ASK OF THE PAST? HOW? WHAT? WHERE? WHEN? WHY? WHO?

CESA 2, UWW, WHS - 2006

A Framework to Enhance and Improve Teaching and Learning

Nikki Mandell and Bobbie Malone

Wisconsin Historical Society Press

Published by the Wisconsin Historical Society Press
Publishers since 1855
www.wisconsinhistory.org

Photos by permission of Janet Elzy (pp. 34, 54), John Hallagan (pp. 78, 79, 104), and the Wisconsin Historical Society (pp. 2, 50, 81, 88).

Printed in Wisconsin, U.S.A.
12 11 10 09 08   2 3 4 5 6

For further information on applying *Thinking like a Historian* and its concepts in the classroom contact:
Nikki Mandell, History Department, University of Wisconsin-Whitewater
mandelln@uww.edu
Bobbie Malone, Office of School Services, Wisconsin Historical Society
bobbie.malone@wisconsinhistory.org

∞ The paper used in this publication meets the minimum requirements of the American National Standard for Information Sciences—Permanence of Paper for Printed Library Materials, ANSI Z39.48-1992.

AUTHORS AND CONTRIBUTORS

Nikki Mandell, earned her Ph.D in history at the University of California-Davis. She is a member of the history department at the University of Wisconsin-Whitewater where she teaches American and global women's history, U.S. business history, U.S. social history and courses in historical methods and research. She is the author of *The Corporation as Family: The Gendering of Corporate Welfare, 1890–1930*. Dr. Mandell is co-chair of her university's Social Studies Council. She served as project director and participating historian in the Teaching American History program that developed and field-tested the Thinking Like a Historian framework.

Bobbie Malone is Director of the Office of School Services at the Wisconsin Historical Society. With a master's degree in elementary education, she taught school for ten years in Louisiana and Texas before taking a doctorate in American History from Tulane University. Dr. Malone is the author of *Rabbi Max Hiller: Reformer, Zionist, Southerner, 1860–1929* and co-author of the textbook *Wisconsin: Our State, Our Story*, which is designed around the Thinking Like a Historian framework. She has authored and edited many other student books and teacher's guides on Wisconsin history for the state's classrooms. She served as a project partner in the Teaching American History program that developed and field-tested the Thinking Like a Historian framework.

Angela Bazan earned her Bachelor's degree in Education from the University of Wisconsin-Whitewater in 1998. Since then, she has been teaching social studies at Deerfield High School, in Deerfield, Wisconsin. Ms. Bazan teaches a wide variety of subjects including US History, Sociology, Diversity, American Government and Advanced Placement American Government. She grew up with a love of history and enjoys fueling that passion by igniting the same interest in her students. Ms. Bazan was a Teaching Fellow with the Teaching American History Teaching program from 2003–2006.

Janet Regina Elzy migrated with her family from Shannon, Mississippi to South Beloit, Illinois, when she was a child. She earned a B.S. in History Education from Northern Illinois University in 1976. Ms. Elzy holds two Masters degrees (in reading and in learning disabilities) and special education certificates for the states of Illinois and Wisconsin. She has instructed special needs students in language arts and social studies for twenty-five years at South Beloit High School in Illinois, and Aldrich Middle School in Beloit, Wisconsin. Ms. Elzy began teaching American history at the middle school level in 2003, the year she became a Teaching American History Teaching Fellow. This TAH experience had a profound effect. Her history classes engage students in critical thinking as "investigators of the past and present." She received a statewide Herb Kohl Teacher of the Year Award in 1994 and a School District of Beloit All Star Teaching Award in 1995.

John Hallagan earned his Bachelors degree from Marquette University in 1975 and his Masters degree in Education from National Louis University in 1993. He has been teaching in Wisconsin public schools for 28 years, the past 12 at Magee Elementary School in the School District of Kettle Moraine in Waukesha. Mr. Hallagan wrote curriculum on immigration history for the American Immigration Law Foundation, runs an annual writers workshop for children and has worked as a teacher advisor with the Teaching American History program for four years. He received the Wisconsin History Teacher of the Year Award from the Gilder Lehrman Foundation in 2005.

Tom Howe earned a Bachelors degree from the University of Wisconsin-Stevens Point and a Masters degree in History from Virginia Tech. He taught middle school and high school history and social studies for 25 years, most recently at Monona Grove High School in Monona, Wisconsin. Mr. Howe teaches an annual Advanced Placement History summer institute for fellow educators and is the author of *The Petersburg Campaign: Wasted Valor, June 15–18, 1864*. He is currently working with the New Teacher Center at the University of California-Santa Cruz, which works to build strong mentor programs. He has received a number of awards, including the Wisconsin Teacher of the Year (1995) and the United States Russia Ukraine Award for Excellence in Teaching (1997). He is most delighted that in 1994 the senior class of Monona Grove High School selected him to receive the first Teacher Appreciation Award.

Tim Keal has taught high school social studies for 8 years at Sun Prairie High School, Sun Pairie, Wisconsin. His classes include world history, U.S. history, economics, international relations and legal studies. Mr. Keal was an active Teaching American History Teaching Fellow for three years and, for the past two years has worked full time as a new teacher mentor with the Sun Prairie Area School District.

Mike McKinnon is Curriculum Coordinator for the Janesville School District, Wisconsin. He earned Bachelors and Masters degrees in History at the University of Wisconsin-Madison. He has been an educator for 40 years, including 18 years teaching high school history and, more recently, as an instructor at Cardinal Stritch University in Milwaukee, Wisconsin. Mr. McKinnon is former President of the Wisconsin Council for the Social Studies and former Chair, Wisconsin Department of Public Instruction Sub-Committee on the Teaching of History. He served as a project partner in the Teaching American History program that developed and field-tested the Thinking Like a Historian framework.

THINKING LIKE A HISTORIAN:
RETHINKING HISTORY INSTRUCTION

We invite you to use *Thinking Like a Historian* to bring history into your classroom or to reenergize your teaching of this crucial discipline in new ways.

A group of experienced Wisconsin historians and educators, representing elementary through university levels, developed and piloted this framework. The Thinking Like a Historian charts which are the centerpiece of *Thinking Like a Historian* were created by condensing into simplified and easily remembered language the combined expertise of the historical profession as expressed in the published standards of the American Historical Association, the Organization of American Historians, the National Council for History Education, the National History Standards and state standards for Wisconsin and California.

The work that follows is the fruit of our thinking and practice grounded in the highest standards of the discipline – designed to stimulate your own thinking, planning, and teaching. Read it as a philosophical and pedagogical guide to history as a discipline. Use it to support curriculum development and professional development. Adapt or draw inspiration from the examples for engaging and effective lessons and classroom activities. Return again and again to the common language of *Thinking Like a Historian* as a foundation that can connect and develop students' curiosity about and understanding of history throughout their school years.

We love history. We're fascinated and enthusiastic about studying and teaching it. As history educators we wholeheartedly embrace the responsibility and opportunity to guide the next generation to think more deeply about the past – to think like historians.

We thank the Teaching American History Teaching Fellows and their students who contributed
to the development of the ideas and practices that follow.

HISTORY DOES MATTER

WHY DOES HISTORY MATTER?

Teaching and learning history matters, and it matters deeply. For many years, teaching history was an important part of the school curriculum. However, the past several decades witnessed its reduction in many school districts into general social studies courses, sometimes taught by those without history degrees. More recently, reductions in social studies programs in some schools are further limiting history teaching and learning.

This state of history education is a significant issue. As a discipline history encourages the sort of deep thinking and reading literacy required in our increasingly complex society. As a subject matter history contains the very essence of who we are and where we come from. By applying a disciplined approach to its study, one can develop a deeper understanding of how nations and cultures came to be. Rather than infusing the study of history into social studies or American civilization courses, school districts should place this important discipline front and center. Only history can give students the information and skills to understand where we've been and why we are as we are.

History is at once interesting, fun, and troubling. Whether we view historically themed films, read historical fiction, visit historical sites, or watch the History Channel, we connect with the struggles and successes of those who have gone before us. History enlivens, informs, and excites both adults and students, and many develop a lifelong love and passion for the subject. Most significantly, the subject is far more than a collection of disconnected dates, facts, and events. **History is a *discipline*: a way of thinking that encourages students to analyze historical evidence, evaluate it, and then demonstrate their understanding of that evidence. Teaching and learning history requires repeated practice with these essential elements of the discipline.** Students who have the opportunity to "do" history engage their passion and enthusiasm for the past while applying the highest levels of critical thinking. Such involved work is well beyond simple memorization of factual material and prepares young people for the kinds of sharpened thinking necessary for a successful adult life.

Beyond a body of knowledge and a way of thinking, the discipline of history helps one make meaning in a chaotic and changing present. The best history courses engage students in the study of historical artifacts and documents–which are often contradictory and muddled—from which they produce original work with nuanced and supported conclusions. As a result of their experience in well-facilitated history courses, such students tend to think more deeply and carefully about topics that matter, including those in their present lives. They're both more hopeful and less likely to be confused by conflicting evidence in our world of "spin." Many start to think in ways that the historian David Hackett Fischer calls "if, then thinking," suggesting that if we wish to make a better world that incorporates the best of the past with fewer of its mistakes, then we must explore what that past world looked like.[1]

[1] David Hackett Fischer, *Historians' Fallacies: Toward a Logic of Historical Thought* (New York: Harper Perennial, 1970), p. 315. Fischer's insight is as valid today as it was *then*, in 1970.

Finally, studying history matters because nearly everyone in our society uses history. Some interpret history for their own purposes or to forward a particular agenda. Some use history as propaganda, hoping to remake the present by remaking popular beliefs about the past. These uses and abuses of history are not a prerogative of any one political or ethical persuasion more than another. In a society fueled by instantaneous information and swirling with historical explanations, students need the power of discernment more than ever before. History education equips students with powerful tools of thought that will allow them to evaluate circumstances and make more learned choices. In a rapidly changing world in which historical ignorance seems to be the rule rather than the exception, there is no more important discipline for our students to practice, at all levels, than history.

LEARNING HISTORY – MAKING SENSE OF THE PAST

History the Way We Used to Learn It:

David Lowenthal writes *The Past is a Foreign Country*. Sam Wineburg writes *Historical Thinking and Other Unnatural Acts*. James Loewen writes *Lies My Teacher Told Me*.[2] The past is foreign? Thinking about the past is unnatural? Worse, teachers lie about it? This is not the way most of us learned history. We were told that history is a large body of indisputable facts about people, places, laws, wars, events, and, most importantly, dates. Teachers and textbooks sought to make the past familiar, not foreign. They taught us that learning history was like learning any other subject, with repeated exposure and forced concentration we would remember the myriad details that made up the body of knowledge known as history. The better we remembered those facts, the better we were at history. At the most challenging levels one was expected to explain what happened in the past by connecting those facts to one another. The accuracy of teachers and textbooks was unquestioned. They had to be right. After all, they were usually the only source of historical information.

History the Way We Should Have Learned It:

The problem with this vision of history is that it fundamentally misrepresents the discipline. History is not akin to stamp collecting. Answering a history question is not like solving a chemistry problem. "Doing history" is not passive. It is not simply memorizing and sequencing facts. **History is a discipline of inquiry and analysis. "Doing history" is an active process of asking good questions about the past, finding and analyzing sources, and drawing conclusions supported by the evidence.** Since this is, as Sam Wineburg writes, "unnatural" for most of us, it's worth considering this basic foundation in more depth.

How Do Historians Learn About the Past?

Most fundamentally, history is *not* the past. It is a study of the past. Studying the past can become quite complicated, but all history begins withquestions. The historian, a teacher, a student wants to know something about the past. She asks "Why did immigrants come to America?" or "Why did the Egyptians build pyramids?" Quite often our curiosity about the past is shaped by our own experiences in the present. Following the rise of dictatorships in the 1930s and the horrors of World War II in the 1940s many historians began asking questions about the roots of American democracy. During the 1960's civil rights activists wondered whether and how earlier generations of Black Americans had struggled for justice. They wanted to know much more about the three centuries of Black experience in America than could be found in the few paragraphs surrounding the Civil War.

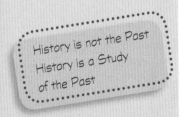
History is not the Past
History is a Study
of the Past

---

[2] David Lowethal, *The Past is a Foreign Country*, (Cambridge, England: Cambridge University Press, 1985); Samuel Wineburg, *Historical Thinking and Other Unnatural Acts*, (Philadelphia: Temple University Press, 2001); James Loewen, *Lies My Teacher Told Me* (New York: The New Press, 1995).

In order to answer a historical question we need information. Depending on the question, and on the vagaries of time, finding that information can range from fairly straightforward to nearly impossible. Part of the ease or difficulty in finding information is related to the kind of information needed. At this stage of the historical process the teacher or student must take on the persona of a "talkative detective." *Why a detective?* History is not a compilation of indisputable facts or statements. History is built on the reasoned evaluation and synthesis of historical evidence. The historical detective searches for, compiles, and sifts through evidence about the past.

Historical evidence comes in two forms: secondary sources and primary sources. **Secondary sources** are comprised of information or explanations *produced after the historical event by people who were not involved* in the historical event. Secondary source information and explanations are based on primary sources and other secondary sources. **Primary sources** are comprised of information or explanations *produced at the time of the event and by people who were involved* in the historical event. Secondary sources provide context, ideas, and information that are essential to understanding the primary sources. The talkative detective needs both.

Why talkative? Finding the "right" sources to answer a historical question is more than a matter of technological competence. In order to find the right sources we must enter into a "dialogue" with the sources by asking many questions of each source we encounter: How does it relate to our historical question? Does it duplicate or contradict other sources? Does it offer new information or perspectives? Do I have a sufficient number and range of sources to be able to answer my question - - do my sources include representation of the relevant voices, interests, issues and/or data?

The conversation moves into a different vein when we turn to evaluating historical sources. Evaluating historical sources is more than a matter of explaining the words or pictures or numbers they contain. Why, when, and by whom was the source created? How do these factors affect the importance and accuracy of the information or ideas contained in the source? Does it reinforce, challenge or deviate from other sources, both secondary and primary? In what ways does it help to answer the historical question? Does it raise additional questions that need to be investigated?

It's worth pausing for a moment to consider how the requisites of the talkative detective differ from what often happens in history education.

Textbook vs Multiple Sources

The omniscient textbook is often the first source of historical information. Textbooks are highly synthesized secondary sources. True, today's textbooks are increasingly punctuated with primary documents. However, primary document sidebars and insets generally serve the synthetic purpose of the texts, either by demonstrating a point made in the narrative or simply by enlivening the visual appeal of the page.

In the past, the next source after the textbook might have been an encyclopedia. Today's students are more likely to "google it" or look for a "wiki." Free-wheeling internet searches yield a hodge-podge of secondary and primary sources of widely varying importance and quality.

These commonly used sources present historical information in the form of seemingly indisputable conclusions or, in the case of some internet sites, in the form of disconnected data. This is distinctly different from the way historians use sources.

How Do Historians Use Historical Sources?

There is a fundamental difference between *looking for answers in the sources and constructing answers from the sources*. Historians construct an understanding of the past from the sources. Constructing answers from the sources, is the final stage of "doing history." At this stage we must put the evidence together to tell a coherent story about the past – a story that answers the historical question. This story, or history, must take into consideration not only multiple sources, but also the multiple and contesting perspectives that shape all human experience. Historians bring those sources into the story as evidence to support and explain their conclusions. This process of historical interpretation gives meaning to the past. It calls on us to explain what matters and why it matters. It also distinguishes history from mere opinion. **Building an interpretation based on evidence is the defining characteristic of history.** Interpretation is the culmination of the work of the talkative detective. Unlike criminal detectives, however, historical detectives do not expect "open and shut" cases or to "wrap up all the loose ends." In some cases, where sources are limited, historical interpretation must be tentative. In some cases, finding answers to one set of questions opens the door to a new set of questions. Successful historical investigations can conclude with questions as well as answers.

Ignoring the interpretive nature of history can lead to *pseudo-history*. One tendency is to present history as uncontested truth (the "lies" James Loewen places at the doorstep of teachers and textbooks). At the other extreme is a tendency to conclude that the absence of a single "right answer" means that all answers are equally valid or relevant. Thus, my historical opinion is as good as your historical opinion. Let's consider these misunderstandings one at a time. First, history is not objective, fixed truth. The process of doing history, the ways in which historians "know" about the past, ensures that history is always constructed. It cannot be static. Why? Our questions about the past change – particularly as our present changes. Americans who lived through the rise of fascism in Europe and militarism in Japan in the 1920s and 1930s wanted to know about the strengths of American democracy. In the 1950s and 1960s many of their children saw a nation of inequality and wanted to know about the nation's long history of democracy denied.

Second, new sources can be discovered. The discovery of long-ignored anti-slavery petitions from the 1830s opened a new window on the role of women in sustaining the anti-slavery movement in the United States. The opening of the archives of the former Soviet Union has spurred a reexamination of a wide array of topics ranging from the Soviet's domestic economy in the 1930s to the global Cold War of the late 20th century. Most recently, a cache of letters from Napoleon Bonaparte, Peter the Great and Mahatma Ghandi were discovered in a laundry room in Switzerland. It is too soon to know what new insights they may reveal.

Reconstructing the Past

▶ Looking for Evidence

▶ Entering into a dialogue with the sources

▶ Analyzing the evidence

▶ Building one's own interpretation supported by the sources

All History is Not Equal

Building Interpretations Based on Evidence

Also, asking different historical questions leads us to interrogate familiar sources in new ways. Curiosity about the strength of American democracy led a generation of post-World War II historians to examine the constitutional system. Curiosity about failures in American democracy led the next generation of historians to examine the constitutional system as well. While the first group was drawn to constitutional provisions establishing federalism and checks and balances, the second group was drawn to constitutional provisions that protected slavery and denied citizenship rights to the majority of the population.

In addition, different people interpret and synthesize the stories told by the sources in different ways, arriving at different answers to similar questions. This does not mean that all historical answers are equally valid or correct. First, some answers are factually incorrect. The Emancipation Proclamation of January 1863, for example, did not free all the slaves. (The Emancipation Proclamation declared an end to slavery only in areas still in rebellion – areas that did not recognize the authority of the United States government and, thus, did not enforce the proclamation.) Second, some answers are not supported by the historical evidence. In this category we might think of the common misconception that the United States entered World War II to end the Holocaust. (The U.S. government did not publicize and chose not to take military action to stop or hinder the Holocaust. Most Americans learned of the Holocaust only as allied troops entered the death camps at the end of the war.) Beyond this, however, there are multiple "right" answers and many legitimate areas of historical disagreement. This brings us to the issue of history as interpretation versus history as opinion or bias.

Historical analysis and interpretation must be grounded in a full consideration of the historical record. The historical record includes all reasonably available secondary and primary sources. Yet, even when we examine the same or similar bodies of evidence, intelligent and thoughtful people can reach supportable, but different conclusions. The key to good history, and the factor that distinguishes historical interpretation from bias or opinion, is the absolute requirement that historical conclusions must be supportable by the historical record AND take into consideration sometimes conflicting perspectives and experiences in that record. Bias slips in when part of the historical evidence is ignored or its importance is discounted without historical justification. This is not history. Opinion slips in when statements are made or conclusions reached without evidence to support those statements or conclusions. This is not history.

Historical Categories of Inquiry:
Finding Patterns and Making Sense of the Past

The process of studying the past (asking questions, analyzing sources and drawing supportable conclusions) is not the only distinguishing mark of the discipline of history. The past is immense, diverse and complex. Studying and understanding that past could be quite daunting, particularly if we described our task as recording everything that ever happened, if we simply asked "What happened?" Fortunately, historians' curiosity about that immensely complex past tends to fall into recognizable patterns of inquiry. These patterns, or what might be called *historical categories of inquiry*, organize both the questions we ask of the past and the answers we construct.[3]

The historical record includes all reasonably available primary and secondary sources

Opinion is not history

Opinion is marked by the absence of historical evidence

Bias is not history

Bias is marked by selective use of the historical record

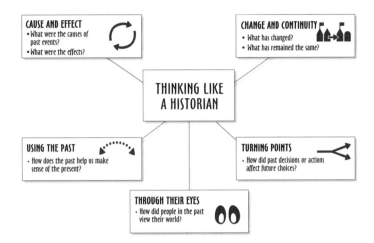

▶ **Cause and effect** is perhaps the most familiar category of historical questioning and explanation. We ask questions about the causes and consequences of past events. Not surprisingly, our answers to these questions, our historical interpretations, take the form of stories about causes and consequences. ↻

▶ We also ask questions about what has changed and what has remained the same over time. Answers to questions about **change and continuity** connect events and give meaning to the chronological sequence of events. 👤👤

▶ In some cases we wonder if the change was so dramatic that the topic of study was a historical **turning point**. By studying the historical record we are able to reach conclusions that some events or developments so dramatically changed a society's ideas, choices and ways of living that some paths of development could no longer be followed and others became more likely or possible. ⤙

▶ In other cases we look to the past as a guide to our present. We want to know about the particular course of events that shaped our present. Or, we are **using the past** to seek guidance in the form of "lessons of history" that can help us grapple with current problems. ⤶

▶ We find it both necessary and fascinating to examine the ways in which people of different times, places and conditions made sense of their world. We consider how their experiences, needs and worldviews affected their actions and the course of events. We try to imagine their world **through their eyes**. 👀

Recognizing the true nature of the historical discipline has significant implications not only for what we want our students to learn, but also for how we teach. Instead of overwhelming ourselves and our students with a plethora of disconnected events, "doing history" allows students to examine the past as a fascinating narrative of human passion, struggle, triumph and tragedy. **We become engaged and help students find meaning in the past when we use discipline-specific skills of historical inquiry and analysis.**

---

[3] The historical categories of inquiry described here and in greater depth throughout this guide encompass the historical thinking skills and historical habits of mind promoted by the major professional historical associations and K–12 national and state history/social studies associations and standards. They were developed by condensing into simplified and easily remembered language the combined expertise of the historical profession as expressed in the published standards of the American Historical Association, the Organization of American Historians, the National Council for History Education, the National History Standards and the standards for Wisconsin and California.

What Should Students Learn? What Should I Teach?

Deciding to invigorate your history curriculum or to introduce history into the curriculum is one thing. Actually doing it is another thing.

Many Voices

Many Voices

- competing demands for classroom and lesson planning time
- standards (school, state, national)
- high stakes testing (school, state, national)
- curriculum content and pacing guides (school, district)
- availability of resources and classroom materials
- students' abilities and prior knowledge
- teachers' abilities and prior knowledge
- new knowledge from professional development and historical scholarship

Changing curriculum is not going to happen in a vacuum. Although the details may vary from teacher to teacher, we begin by acknowledging the multiple factors that affect what history we teach, how we teach history, and how our students learn history. At times these can seem overwhelming.

Trying to balance and satisfy these many voices could lead one to question whether there is space for innovation or new initiatives. **Yet, we do make choices every day about what to teach and how to teach. The ideas and examples that follow are about those choices.** They provide a framework and tools for making informed and supportable choices. They provide a framework and tools for doing a better job at what we already do, or want to do.

Coverage versus Depth

One of the first choices that shapes history curriculum is often posed as a trade off between coverage and depth.

▶ **Coverage** seems to promise that students will be exposed to and cognizant of the many historical people, places, events, dates, institutions, and documents that are deemed essential to an educated citizenry.

▶ **Depth** seems to promise that students will become engaged as they develop historical skills and enduring understandings of a limited number of significant people or events.

What are you teaching this week?

Coverage	Depth
"I'm teaching Chapter 3."	"I'm teaching how the Constitution changed during the 19th century."
"The students are doing a worksheet on pp. 35–45."	"The students are studying the consequences of WWI."

The debate between coverage and depth is insoluble and misguided. It is insoluble because there is no silver bullet or one right answer. It is misguided because it presumes that each of these approaches, coverage and depth, are possible without the other. In reality, even the shallowest coverage approach requires that some things be "left out." Even the most fast-paced coverage approach pauses or slows down at "key events." Similarly, in-depth study of a historical topic requires attention to historical context. Setting historical context requires covering broad developments as well as specific people, events and patterns that preceded, overlapped, and, in some cases, followed the topic of in-depth study. We cannot make sense of any historical topic unless we consider it within its historical context. Thus, the question is not: Which of these, coverage or depth, should take priority? **The question is: Which historical topics warrant more in-depth and which historical topics warrant less in-depth study?**

Thinking Like a Historian as a Guide to Lesson and Curriculum Planning

What does it mean to "warrant" more or less in-depth study? How can a teacher make this decision? In the absence of better criteria, these choices can become disconnected from the primary objective of deepening and broadening students' understanding of history. The *Thinking Like a Historian framework* **TLH** can serve as a guide to making informed decisions that are directly connected to significant course themes, driving questions and key understandings.

Deciding which historic topics warrant more or less in-depth study

Relevant but **not** sufficient

- I have the materials.
- It's the curriculum that was handed to me.
- Students really like it.
- I found it on the web/in a teacher guide

Relevant **and** sufficient

- History-specific standard of measure. Which history matters?
- Pedagogically-specific standard of measure. How will students learn best?
- Historical Literacy: Does it further students' understanding of history as a discipline of inquiry and analysis? Does it further students' understanding of history as meaningful and exciting stories about the past?

The *Thinking Like a Historian framework* **TLH** supports choices that move beyond commonly cited explanations (my students like it, I have the materials) to ensure that history education is both meaningful and engaging.

TLH provides a common language
        —TAH Teaching Fellow

Historical literacy incorporates the *historical process* (the disciplinary skills and procedures that historians use to study the past) and *historical categories of inquiry* (the conceptual patterns that historians use to make sense of the past). These two aspects of historical literacy are embedded in the standards that influence history education today. However, this is not readily apparent. The text of most history standards combine elements of both *historical process* and *historical categories of inquiry* without distinguishing their relationship to one another. As a consequence, the distinctive elements and qualities of the historical process and historical analysis are not clear. **The *Thinking Like a Historian* framework** **TLH** **presented here is unique because it purposefully separates and investigates these crucial aspects of historical literacy.** By doing so, **TLH** empowers both teachers and students to become more historically literate.

The relationship between these two aspects of historical literacy is graphically represented on the **TLH** chart by the outer banner and the inner panel. The outer banner identifies the key elements of the *historical process*. The inner panel identifies the key *historical categories of inquiry*.

▶ **Outer Banner:** *Historical process* is the history-specific ways of learning about the past: How do we know? Historical process is the way we investigate the past.

▶ **Inner Panel:** *Historical categories of inquiry* are ways of organizing inquiry and analysis of the myriad people, events, and ideas of the past. These categories of historical inquiry and analysis provide the patterns that help us make sense of the past.

The outer banner and inner panel are in continuous, dynamic interaction with one another. The outer banner wraps around the entire poster because the historical process of studying the past informs what we can know about the past. The inner panel is relevant to all stages of the historical process because we use these categories of inquiry to formulate the questions we ask of the past and to determine what matters and why it matters as we construct a historical interpretation.

Understanding the elements of historical literacy is essential to teaching historical literacy. This section of the guide explains the key elements of *historical process* and *historical categories of inquiry*. It includes rubrics you can use to assess the historical literacy of curriculum plans, classroom activities and student learning. (Full page copies of these charts and rubrics are included in Section 4: Resources.)

Historical Process

+

Historical Categories
of Inquiry

=

Historical Literacy

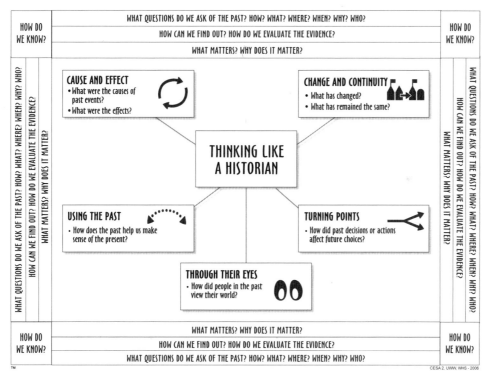

[Full size chart available in Resource section]

Important points to keep in mind as you read on:

▶ *Historical literacy cannot be separated from "content."* Content is essential and inescapable. The historical process requires the evaluation and analysis of historical evidence (historical facts, broadly defined). Content supplies the building blocks for historical interpretation.

▶ *Some* **TLH** *processes and concepts are easier to communicate than others.* For example, most teachers can imagine ways to explore cause or effect with children of all ages. Some are more difficult and can be misunderstood. For example, many teachers may wonder whether young children can make connections between past and present. However....

▶ *Learners at all levels can engage in all stages of the historical process and they can use all historical categories of inquiry.* Naturally 3rd graders will not master these at the same level or complexity as 10th graders. Teaching historical literacy requires developmentally appropriate classroom activities and lessons for all learners. See Section 3 for examples.

How Do We Know? – Historical Process

The *historical process* is the procedure that historians use to learn about the past. Historians use this disciplinary process whenever they study the past. It consists of three steps. Although it must necessarily look and feel a bit different in the classroom, teaching and learning historical literacy requires the same three steps.

1. Asking questions about the past
2. Gathering sources and Evaluating the evidence in those sources
3. Drawing conclusions, supported by the evidence, that answer the questions

HOW DO WE KNOW?	WHAT QUESTIONS DO WE ASK OF THE PAST? HOW? WHAT? WHERE? WHEN? WHY? WHO?	HOW DO WE KNOW?
	HOW CAN WE FIND OUT? HOW DO WE EVALUATE THE EVIDENCE?	
	WHAT MATTERS? WHY DOES IT MATTER?	

❓ Questions

History is a study of the past, it is not the past itself. That study of the past, history, begins with questions. Historians and others ask a wide range of questions about the past. Yet, as we examine those questions, we can discern certain patterns. Helping students understand this is an essential element of history education.

1. History begins with questions – something we want to know, something we are curious about.

2. Questions about the past generally fall into one of the five historical categories of inquiry.

3. Some questions are better than others. The most interesting and meaningful questions recognize that the human experience in the past was as complex as the present. Historical events unfolded as different people, groups and institutions with different experiences, needs, ideas and degrees of power interacted with one another.

Rubric for teachers [excerpted from Instruction and Assessment Planning Rubric, Resources section]

Use rubrics for self-reflection, evaluating lesson plans, classroom activities, and assessment.

TLH HISTORICAL PROCESS	Level: 4	Level: 3	Level: 2	Level: 1
❓ **Questions** • Some questions are better than others. The most interesting and meaningful questions recognize that the human experience in the past was as complex as the present. • Historical events unfolded as different people, groups and institutions with different experiences, needs, ideas and degrees of power interacted	• requires attention to multiple perspectives or experiences • requires significant manipulation and use of evidence to support answer • requires analysis that incorporates two or more TLH categories • requires consideration of historical context and change over time	• requires attention to multiple perspectives or experiences • requires some explanation or manipulation of evidence • requires some use of evidence to support answer • may call for compare/contrast or before/after statements • may not require consideration of historical context	• requires attention to only one perspective or experience • little explanation of evidence required • may not require consideration of historical context	• can be answered with simple yes/no or T/F or fill in the blank • seeks factual responses that require little to no explanation or integration of evidence • does not require consideration of historical context

Evidence

In order to answer historical questions we need information. This information, the historical evidence, comes from **secondary sources** (such as books, documentaries, lectures, textbooks and maps) and **primary sources** (such as letters, newspapers, speeches, diaries, treaties, photographs, oral interviews, and census reports). Historical evidence contains facts about the past. Facts are not history. Helping students understand this is an essential element of history education.

1. Facts are the building blocks and supporting evidence we need in order to answer the really interesting and meaningful historical questions.

2. Not all historical sources are equal. It is necessary to consider ways in which a number of factors may affect the validity of each source. Among these are: the creator of the source, the creator's perspective and knowledge about events, the purpose the source was created, and the intended audience for the source.

3. Multiple sources are needed in order to fully understand the complexity and importance of any historical event, era, or person, or group. "Dumbing it down" can lead to incorrect, distorted or mythical conclusions.

4. Sources must provide information about both historical context and the topic under study.

Rubric for teachers [excerpted from Instruction and Assessment Planning Rubric, Resources section]

Use rubrics for self-reflection, evaluating lesson plans, classroom activities, and assessment.

TLH HISTORICAL PROCESS	Level: 4	Level: 3	Level: 2	Level: 1
Evidence Historical sources are not all equal. • It is necessary to consider factors that affect the validity of each source. • Among these are: the creator of the source, the creator's perspective and knowledge about events, the purpose the source was created, and the intended audience • Multiple sources are needed in order to fully understand the complexity and importance of any historical event, era, person, or group. "Dumbing it down" can lead to incorrect, distorted or mythical conclusions.	• uses multiple primary and secondary sources representing a variety of perspectives and/or types of information • identifies author/creator of sources and requires assessment of effect of this on validity and perspective • requires deep analysis of information, motivation and perspectives expressed in sources • requires comparison/contrasts with other sources as part of each source analysis	• uses multiple sources • generally includes combination of primary and secondary sources, although may use one or two of each • identifies author/creator of source, although may not consider the effect of this on validity, perspective or how to evaluate the source(s) • requires some consideration of information, motivation and perspective expressed in source	• uses one or two sources, generally secondary; source(s) presents its account of the past as "authoritative uncontested truth" • no attention to evaluating validity or perspective of the source(s)	• uses one, generally secondary source (textbook, encyclopedia) • no attempt to evaluate validity, perspective or credibility of source

⚖️ *Interpretation*

The final and essential step in doing history is historical interpretation. Historical interpretation answers a historical question using the reasonably available historical record (primary and secondary sources). Helping students understand this is an essential element of history education.

1. Whether the question is stated explicitly or not, all secondary sources are examples of historical interpretation.

2. Although the past cannot change, history does change. History is a study of the past. New questions, new sources or new understandings of familiar sources and/or new explanations or syntheses of the evidence lead to new interpretations.

3. All historical interpretations are not equal. Some are better than others. Some are wrong. Some are misleading. (see discussion of bias and opinion vs interpretation in Section 1)

4. The quality of one's historical interpretation depends on the questions one asks, the breadth and depth of the sources one uses, and the sophistication of one's analysis and synthesis of the sources in support of the answer to the historical question.

Rubric for teachers [excerpted from Instruction and Assessment Planning Rubric, Resources section]

Use rubrics for self-reflection, evaluating lesson plans, classroom activities, and assessment.

TLH HISTORICAL PROCESS	Level: 4	Level: 3	Level: 2	Level: 1
⚖️ **Interpretation** Historical interpretations are not all equal • Some are better than others. • Some are wrong. • Some are misleading.	• analysis and synthesis are fully supported by ideas, concepts and information from multiple sources • explains historical context and reasons for change over time • accounts for multiple perspectives and experiences • makes connections and explains relationships between people, events, ideas, places • explanation of significance is clear and recognizes complex connections between people, events, concepts and/or past and present.	• explains how and why (as well as what, when, where, who) • may concentrate on presenting a linked chronology or juxtaposing two different perspectives • uses some evidence from sources to support explanations • may recognize, but does not analyze reasons for differences, similarities, change over time • offers generalized explanation of significance	• primarily addresses what, when, where, who • responses are low on Bloom's taxonomy (identify and describe) • little use of evidence to support response	• responses are at recall level of Bloom's taxonomy • does not use evidence to support responses

Historical Categories of Inquiry

Historical categories of inquiry are ways of organizing investigation and interpretation of the past. They encapsulate key patterns of historical inquiry, analysis and synthesis. Regardless of the specific time or place, historians' curiosity about the past (questions) and their conclusions about what matters and why (interpretations) are connected to these categories:

1. Cause and Effect

2. Change and Continuity

3. Turning Points

4. Using the Past

5. Through Their Eyes

Teachers can use these historical categories of inquiry to connect the study of one period, place or event to other periods, places or events. Pedagogically, this serves two important purposes:

• First, continuous use of these historical categories provides a way to integrate students' prior knowledge. In this respect, the **TLH** *framework can serve as the foundation of a spiraled and sequenced curriculum,* even as the "content" topics shift from the American Revolution to the Civil War or from state history to ancient civilizations.

• Second, continuous use of these historical categories *builds a common language that students can use to direct their curiosity and exploration of any historical topic.* As students learn to think about the past according to these disciplinary patterns they are freed from notions of history as a collection of facts. History becomes a way of thinking about the past, rather than details to be recalled as history teachers and tests demand.

The **TLH** questions in the following pages explain and expand on the **TLH** Chart and **TLH** Question Chart below. [Full size charts available in Resources section]

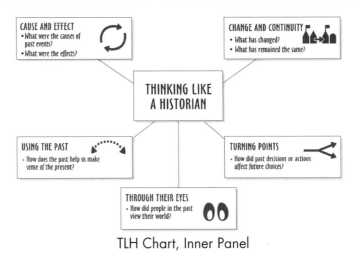

TLH Chart, Inner Panel

CAUSE AND EFFECT	CHANGE AND CONTINUITY	TURNING POINTS	USING THE PAST	THROUGH THEIR EYES
What were the causes of past events?	What has changed?	How did past decisions or actions affect future choices?	How does the past help us make sense of the present?	How did people in the past view their world?
What were the effects?	What has remained the same?	• How did decisions or actions narrow or eliminate choices for people?	• How is the past similar to the present?	• How did their worldview affect their choices and actions?
• Who or what made change happen?	• Who has benefited from this change? And why?		• How is the past different from the present?	• What values, skills and forms of knowledge did people need to succeed?
• Who supported change?	• Who has not benefited? And why?	• How did decisions or actions significantly transform people's lives?	• What can we learn from the past?	
• Who did not support change?				
• Which effects were intended?				
• Which effects were accidental?				
• How did events affect people's lives, community, and the world?				

TLH Question Chart

Teachers and students can use these questions as starting points to guide their inquiry and analysis of historical topics. The generic nature of these questions captures the common threads that underpin historical knowledge and make it possible to explore similarities, differences and trends across historical time and place. These questions are purposefully broad in order to suggest the range of issues that can be explored through each analytical category.

Teachers and students can use these **TLH** questions as prompts or starting points for elaborating more detailed or topic-specific questions. For example, a sub-set of the Cause and Effect question, "Who or what made change happen?" might be: "How did economic conditions affect what happened?" or "How did the new law affect world trade?" A sub-set of the Turning Points question "How did decisions or actions significantly transform people's lives?" might be: "How did the arrival of millions of immigrants between 1880–1920 transform American cities?" or "How did U.S. foreign policy change as a consequence of World War II?"

⟳ *Cause and Effect*

Although the terms sound simple, the causes and effects of historical events can be very complex. In order to investigate and develop a meaningful understanding of historical cause and effect students need to look beyond single factors. They need to explore the full complexity of the past, recognizing that every event was effected by and affected multiple groups of people and institutions.

We can never know, and certainly we cannot teach, about every person, group or institution. However, full consideration of key groups and their different ideas, motives, actions, and experiences must be part of the story if we are to develop an understanding of the past that reasonably explains what happened and why. This demands attention to causes and effects that are readily apparent as well as those that are more subtle although no less significant, to causes and effects connected to the period immediately surrounding an event as well as those that unfolded over long periods of time, and to causes and effects that were intended as well as to those that were unintended. The following questions open pathways to deeper inquiry and analysis: [excerpted from **TLH** Question Chart, Resources section]

What were the causes of past events?

- Who or what made change happen?
- Who supported change?
- Who did not support change?

What were the effects?

- Which effects were intended?
- Which effects were accidental?
- How did events affect people's lives, community, and the world?

Rubric for teachers [excerpted from Instruction and Assessment Planning Rubric, Resources section]

Use rubrics for self-reflection, evaluating lesson plans, classroom activities, and assessment.

TLH CATEGORIES OF INQUIRY	Level: 4	Level: 3	Level: 2	Level: 1
⟳ **Cause & Effect** Long term causes and/or effects include: • events, actions or changing patterns of life occurring years or decades before or after the topic of study • existing cultural values or beliefs • political or economic systems that set limits on people's choices	• distinguishes multiple causes and/or multiple effects, including both obvious and intended and more subtle and unintended causes and effects, as well as long and short term causes and effects • recognizes that different groups were affected in different ways	• distinguishes multiple causes of an event and/or multiple effects of an event, including long and short term • recognizes that different groups were affected in different ways	• addresses multiple causes and/or effects • but limited to short term and obvious/intended only	• addresses only one or two causes and/or effects • generally limited to short term and obvious/intended only

Change and Continuity

Historical chronology is a distinguishing characteristic of history. Historical chronology differs from other chronologies. For example, the physical sciences include cyclical chronologies (seasons of the year) and repeatable chronologies (experiments that can be reproduced in accordance with a recognized method). Historical chronology is neither cyclical nor repeatable. **Rather, historical chronology is focused on change over time.** Historical chronology marks the passage of time *and* the passage of people and events of that time.

Certainly there are patterns in human experience that reappear across time and space. Understanding these patterns is part of, but not the entirety of understanding historical chronology. More importantly, historians seek to understand how and why things change. In order to do this successfully, they must consider that different people and groups participate in and experience the same events in different ways. The following questions open pathways to deeper inquiry and analysis: [excerpted from **TLH** Question Chart, Resources section]

What has changed?
What has remained the same?

- Who has benefited from this change? And why?
- Who has not benefited from this change? And why?

Rubric for teachers [excerpted from Instruction and Assessment Planning Rubric, Resources section]

Use rubrics for self-reflection, evaluating lesson plans, classroom activities, and assessment.

TLH CATEGORIES OF INQUIRY	Level: 4	Level: 3	Level: 2	Level: 1
Change & Continuity • The past does not repeat itself. • Some aspects of the human experience are constant over long periods of time.	• clearly links change AND continuity to a specific event or series of developments • addresses change and continuity on multiple levels including social, economic, political and/or cultural and over both long and short time periods, trends or patterns • recognizes that different groups were affected in different ways	• clearly links change AND continuity to a specific event or series of developments; • addresses change and continuity in terms of both long and short time periods, trends or patterns • may focus on only one type (social, economic, political or cultural); • recognizes that different groups were affected in different ways	• clearly links change AND continuity to a specific event or series of developments • limited attention to either long OR short time periods and/or focus on only one type (social, economic, political or cultural)	• addresses change OR continuity, failing to address both • connection of change or continuity to the specific event or series of developments not clear

⟨ *Turning Points*

Some change is so dramatic that historians refer to these points of new departure as
historical turning points. A turning point signifies a profound change in one or more of
the major arenas of human experience (political, social, economic or cultural/intellectual).
**Turning points are characterized by change of such magnitude that the course of
individual experiences and societal development begins to follow a new trajectory,
shaped by a new set of possibilities and constraints.**

In some cases, people recognize that they are in the midst of a historical turning point. The
dropping of the atomic bombs at the end of World War II is a relatively recent example
of this. (Of course, recognizing that one is living through a historical turning point does
not mean that one can predict the outcomes of that turning point.) In other cases, people
do not recognize that shifting events are remaking their world. Only the rare American in
1776 might have guessed that their War of Independence was the opening battle in an
"age of revolutions" that overthrew the *Ancien Regime* in France and European empires
in the Americas. The following questions open pathways to deeper inquiry and analysis:
[excerpted from **TLH** Question Chart, Resources section]

How did past decisions or actions affect future choices?

• How did decisions or actions narrow or eliminate choices for people?
• How did decisions or actions significantly transform people's lives?

Rubric for teachers [excerpted from Instruction and Assessment Planning Rubric, Resources section]

Use rubrics for self-reflection, evaluating lesson plans, classroom activities, and assessment.

TLH CATEGORIES OF INQUIRY	Level: 4	Level: 3	Level: 2	Level: 1
⟨ **Turning Points** New set of parameters or new path of social, political or economic development For example: • end of slavery • rise of waged labor • rise of U.S. as a global power • emergence of Victorian norms of womanhood and manhood	• recognizes both major historical events (wars, industrial revolution) AND less obvious events (migration and demography, social or cultural changes, technological or medical changes) as "turning points" • explains why or how these developments established a new set of parameters or established a different path of historical development	• recognizes major, traditionally-studied historical events as "turning points" (wars, industrial revolution, economic depression) • explains why or how these events established a new set of parameters or established a different path of historical development	• recognizes major, traditionally-studied historical events as "turning points" (wars, industrial revolution, economic depression) • does not explain why or how these events established a new set of parameters or established a different path of historical development	• does not identify any historical changes or event as a "turning point" which set a new course or new set of parameters

◢ ••••••• ◣ *Using the Past*

Drawing lessons from the past can be a powerful way to make sense of the present and to inform decisions about the future. One can also use the past for less immediate purposes. Historians use their understanding of one historical event to explain the background to or raise questions about another historical event. Using the past in both ways, to inform choices in the present and to better understand events in the past, makes history relevant. Using the past invests history with meaning.

At the same time, using the past responsibly is fraught with enormous challenges. Since history does not repeat itself, no past event is a perfect guide to later events or future actions. **Using the past responsibly requires finding the useable past.** In order to find the useable past we must be able to discriminate between those events and aspects of the past that are relevant to and those that are not relevant to the event under study.

Some historical similarities are comparable, others are not. For example, comparing divorce rates in 1890 to those in 1990 would lead to false conclusions about the stability of the American nuclear family. Why? The significant causes of family instability in 1890 were death and desertion, not divorce. Although many Americans opposed U.S. involvement in both the Philippine-American War and World War I, the former is more relevant if one is trying to understand public opposition to the American War in Vietnam. Why? Guerilla warfare and charges of imperial intent fueled popular discontent with both of these wars. The following questions open pathways to deeper inquiry and analysis: [excerpted from **TLH** Question Chart, Resources section]

How does the past help us make sense of the present?

- How is the past similar to the present?
- How is the past different from the present?
- What can we learn from the past?

Rubric for teachers [excerpted from Instruction and Assessment Planning Rubric, Resources section]

Use rubrics for self-reflection, evaluating lesson plans, classroom activities, and assessment.

TLH CATEGORIES OF INQUIRY	Level: 4	Level: 3	Level: 2	Level: 1
◢••••◣ Using the Past Historians only use parts of the past. Need to discriminate between which parts of past events are comparable and which are not by considering: • What are the parallels or similarities? • What is different? • All similarities are not "useable" for comparative purposes	• distinguishes elements of, or patterns in, past events or periods that are similar to AND that are different from a contemporary situation • using knowledge of that past event or period draws supportable conclusions about the contemporary situation	• traces developmental relationship, over time and space, between past events or patterns and contemporary events or patterns; • recognizes factors that have contributed to changes over time in the parallel event or pattern	• recognizes similarities and/or differences between past events and contemporary issues, but makes simple, linear connections that jump over decades/centuries of time without addressing impact of intervening developments	• makes no connections between past events or trends and contemporary life

👀 *Through Their Eyes*

This can be the most fascinating aspect of historical study. It opens a door to understanding both what all humanity shares in common and the many ways in which we are different. It brings us closest to the real lives of real people in the past. What did their world look like? How did they spend their days and nights? Who was in their family and what were they expected to do? What motivated them to act in the ways they did? How did they deal with the problems of their day?

This can also be the most misunderstood aspect of historical study. **Exploring these and many other questions can deepen historical understanding only if we remember that we are observers of the past, not actors in the past.** We can never be an African-American woman watching her children dragged away by slave traders. We can never be an Italian boy preparing to leave the only home he knows to join his father in a far away place called New York. We have a different set of beliefs, expectations, desires, fears, opportunities and experiences than they did. What is logical or rational to us may have been impossible, inconceivable, or foolhardy in their world – and vice versa. Ignoring this leads to errors of "presentism."

What we can do is to "listen" to the voices of the past without preconceptions. We must let people of the past begin *and* end their own sentences. In order to understand why people thought and acted in the way they did in the past we need to see the world as they saw it. We need to see their world through their eyes. The following questions open pathways to deeper inquiry and analysis: [excerpted from **TLH** Question Chart, Resources section]

How did people in the past view their world?

- How did their worldview affect their choices and actions?
- What values, skills and forms of knowledge did people need to succeed?

Rubric for teachers [excerpted from Instruction and Assessment Planning Rubric, Resources section]

Use rubrics for self-reflection, evaluating lesson plans, classroom activities, and assessment.

TLH CATEGORIES OF INQUIRY	Level: 4	Level: 3	Level: 2	Level: 1
👀 **Through their eyes** • Seek to understand the world view of historical actors and the ways this affected their choices and actions. • Avoid presentism (evaluating the past according to present-day beliefs and actions)	• draws interpretive connections between the ways in which different groups of historical actors understood "their present" (as in level 3) and the ways they responded to the problems, opportunities and choices that confronted them	• recognizes that historical actors brought multiple perspectives to the same event, reflecting differences in class, gender, race/ethnicity, region, religion, age, education, past experiences • does not necessarily connect these perspectives to significant historical developments	• recognizes that people's lives in the past differed in significant way from contemporary, 21st century, life; inc. gender roles, class divisions, personal and national goals, racial/ethnic attitudes, material standards of life • may connect this to personal goals or actions	• uses contemporary values and knowledge [early 21st century] to explain or make sense of past actions or decisions

The study of history always begins with questions. Good history teaching also begins with questions.

- What do my students know when they arrive in my classroom?
- What should my students know when they leave my classroom?
- Why should they know it? Why does it matter?
- How can I help them learn what they should know?

Connecting what we do in the classroom on a day-to-day basis to larger lesson, unit and curriculum goals can be a challenge in any subject area. This section offers ideas and examples of ways you can use the Thinking Like a Historian **TLH** framework to make those connections and build your students' historical literacy.

CURRICULUM AND LESSON PLANNING

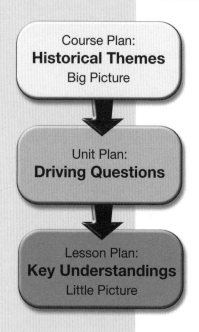

As discussed earlier, historians become "talkative detectives" in order to answer their historical questions. [See Learning History-Making Sense of the Past, Section 1] Teachers should engage in a similar type of conversation in order to ensure that history curriculum and lessons promote historical literacy. In this case, the conversation needs to examine ways to connect what will happen in the classroom on a daily or weekly basis to larger unit, school year and developmental objectives for history learning. The challenge is to establish curriculum and lessons that clearly identify and connect history specific learning objectives at each of these levels. The Curriculum Planning chart, which has three tiers, serves as a guide and overview. [Full size worksheet available in Resources section]

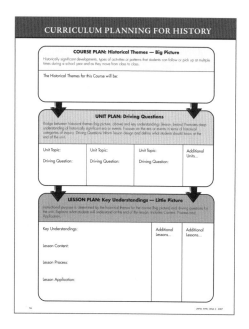

CURRICULUM PLANNING

Choosing Historical Themes – The Big Picture

Anyone who teaches history quickly realizes that there is an overwhelming amount of content. Even if there is a clearly articulated curriculum, teachers must make conscious decisions about what to teach. **Knowing that a class must study the American Civil War or Ancient Rome does not, by itself, tells us what students should know about that topic.** By asking – and answering – questions about the past, teachers are able to prioritize content and present lessons that provoke inquiry. Perhaps the most important question is: "Why does it matter?"

"Why does it Matter?" directs our attention to historical significance.
Historically significant people, events and ideas can be connected to larger historical stories. Historians sometimes call these larger historical stories "themes." Historians construct historical themes as they study the past. They make sense of and find meaning in the details of the past by connecting people, events and ideas to themes that cross time and space.

> Historically significant people, events and ideas can be connected to larger historical stories or "themes."

What are the historically significant themes? What are the larger stories that cross time and space? Historians and teachers of history may arrive at different answers to these questions. As teachers we need to choose historical themes that have scope and sequence across the school year and from year to year. **Themes are historically significant stories that students can follow or pick up at multiple times during a school year and as they move from class to class.** Themes are the building blocks for a history scope and sequence that can draw on student learning in prior units or classes and extend student learning for later units or classes.

Choosing themes should be the first step in curriculum planning. For those familiar with the process of Backward Design, this is the history-specific equivalent of choosing overarching understandings.[1]

> When historians use the term "time" they mean the passage of chronological time as measured by days, months, years, centuries, millennia. When historians use the term "space" they mean geographical place, as defined by village, city, countryside, region, nation, empire.

---

[1] Grant Wiggins and Jay McTighe, *Understanding by Design*, (Alexandria: Association for Supervision and Curriculum Development, 2005).

```
┌────────────────────────────────────────────────────────────────────┐
│              COURSE PLAN: Historical Themes — Big Picture             │
│                                                                      │
│  Historically significant developments, types of activities or patterns that students can follow or pick up at multiple │
│  times during a school year and as they move from class to class.    │
│ ──────────────────────────────────────────────────────────────────── │
│                                                                      │
│  The Historical Themes for this Course will be:                      │
│                                                                      │
│                                                                      │
│                                                                      │
│                                                                      │
└────────────────────────────────────────────────────────────────────┘
```

[Excerpted from Curriculum Planning for History Worksheet, Resources section]

How does one go about choosing themes? To get started its important to remember that:

- **History encompasses change over time.** Thus, historically significant themes focus attention on *aspects of the past that underwent or contributed to significant change over time.*

- **History encompasses all aspects of the human experience.** Thus, historically significant themes focus attention on *economic, social, political, cultural, intellectual, and/or technological developments.*

- **History encompasses the experiences of all people.** Thus, historically significant themes focus attention on *everyday life, social customs, powerful people and groups and people and groups with little or no power.*

- **Identifying and selecting historically significant themes that meet these criteria requires historical knowledge.** In addition to one's own historical knowledge, *teachers should take full advantage of the collective wisdom of historians.* Historians, often in collaboration with classroom teachers and education administrators, have produced a number of resources designed specifically to identify and explain significant historical themes for K–12 education. *Rather than reinventing the wheel, you can use the three criteria above to select historically significant themes from these well-vetted sources.* [See "Starting Places: Finding Historical Themes" below.]

- **Some state and school district history standards incorporate significant historical themes.** Often these coincide with recommendations made in the sources listed below because the standard-writers consulted these well-vetted sources.

Starting Places: Finding Historical Theme

Note: Some of the themes identified in these sources are immediately transferable to the classroom. Some of the themes may need to be narrowed or expanded for courses focused on a particular historical era or region.

▶ *Lessons from History: Essential Understandings and Historical Perspectives Students Should Acquire*, identifies and explains four major narrative themes for U.S. and World History. The themes for U.S. History, for example, are: (1) The gathering of the many peoples who have made up and are still transforming U.S. society; (2) The economic and technological transformation of the United States; (3) Change and continuity in American culture, thought and education, in religious and moral values; (4) Democracy's evolution in the United States and our Changing global role.[2]

▶ *Building a History Curriculum*, describes up to a dozen central themes for U.S., Western and World History. The eight themes for U.S. history, for example, include: (1) The evolution of American political democracy, its ideas, institution, and practices...; (2) The development of the American economy; geographic and other forces at work; the role of the frontier and agriculture; the impact of technological change and urbanization...; (3) The gathering of people and cultures from many countries, and the several religious traditions....; (4) The changing role of the United States in the outside world; relations between domestic affairs and foreign policy...[3]

▶ American Historical Association pamphlet series on teaching. Pamphlets on specific historical topics explain the major themes that animate historical study of that topic, provide succinct discussion of those themes and include recommendations for further resources. Topics include African-American history, immigration history and women's history, among others.[4]

▶ *Magazine of History*, a publication of the Organization of American Historians, focuses on a different historical topic in each issue. Introductory articles discuss the significant historical themes and historical questions that animate study of that issue's topic.[5]

▶ *History Now*, an on-line publication of the Gilder Lehrman Institute, also highlights a specific historical topic in each issue. Articles explain historical themes related to that topic as well as connections between those topical and larger historical themes.[6]

▶ [Additional resources listed in Resource section]

[2] National Center for History in the Schools, *Lessons from History: Essential Understandings and Historical Perspectives Students Should Acquire*, (Los Angeles: National Center for History in the Schools, 1992), pp. 28–40. This companion volume to the National Standards in History is a treasure trove of ideas, information and explanations about topics and themes for both U.S. and World History.

[3] National Council for History Education, *Building a History Curriculum: Guidelines for Teaching History in Schools*, (Westlake, Ohio: National Center for History Education, 2003), pp. 12–15.

[4] Titles for the teaching pamphlets as well as additional sources on teaching history can be found in the on-line publications catalog for the American Historical Association. http://www.historians.org/pubs/overview.cfm [accessed 8/15/07]

[5] Organization of American Historians, *Magazine of History*. Published bi-monthly. Subscription information available at: http://www.oah.org/pubs/magazine/ [accessed 8/15/07]

[6] Gilder Lehrman Institute, *History Now*. Published quarterly. Accessible on-line at: http://www.historynow.org/past.html [accessed 8/15/07]

Course Plan:
Historical Themes
Big Picture

Unit Plan:
Driving Questions

Lesson Plan:
Key Understandings
Little Picture

Examples from the Field *Choosing Historical Themes*

• *State History: Elementary School*

When I plan the curriculum for fourth grade social studies I need to consider all the social studies content strands pertaining to Wisconsin's geography, history, economy, culture, and government. I give focus and direction to this broad spectrum of content by putting history at the center.

I develop course themes for fourth grade social studies directly from TLH: *What matters?* and *Why does it matter?* I address this issue of significance by developing overarching questions about the past that will help my students make sense of the present (using the past). These thematic questions purposefully incorporate multiple categories of historical inquiry: When did people come? Why did they stay? Why did they leave? (cause and effect) What did the people of the past do to survive? (through their eyes) What has changed? What has remained the same? How have people's attitudes changed over time? (change and continuity)

When did people come here? Why did they stay? Why did they leave? These questions allow me and my students to make connections between the ancient people who migrated here during the last Ice Age, the European explorers thousands of years later, immigrant settlers during the 1800s coupled with the forced relocation of Native peoples, and urban migration during the Industrial Revolution. Seeking answers to these big questions helps my students develop a skeletal understanding of who came to this land before us. Using the past, students can analyze the factors that brought their own ancestors to this place. Turning points such as the Black Hawk War and the Trail of Tears are events that illustrate how others were forced out of their homelands, and compelled to create new communities and means of survival.

TOPIC: State History

Historical Themes:

- This land's native people survived thousands of years on natural resources
- Early European explorers, traders & immigrants influenced change
- Government created the state of Wisconsin and forced natives to relocate
- Economic changes tied to natural resources & technological advances
- National conflicts impacted Wisconsin

What did the people of the past do to survive? This big question leads young historians to initially examine archeological evidence that points to hunting and gathering. My students make connections to this theme as they read historical accounts of 18th century fur trading, 19th century lumber industry, and the impact of advances in agriculture and industrialization that preceded the current leading industry, tourism. Learning about the change and continuity of our economic past enables students to articulate thoughtful responses to the questions, *What has changed?* and *What has remained the same?*

How have Wisconsin people's attitudes changed over time? Striving to understand how the people of the past perceived the world around them requires an emotional detachment on the part of historians. To think like historians, my students learn to refrain from using contemporary values to judge historical attitudes in an effort to better understand the past. They need to avoid presentism. We look at the role of government in the shaping of our state and note that one reason the first state constitution was voted down in 1846 was because it gave women the right to vote. Two years later, the second state constitution was ratified without that provision. While such an attitude seems repugnant today, it does help to explain why women have had and continue to have less voice in our government than men.

 • Modern United States History: High School

 Through much of my teaching career, and like many history teachers who wrestle with how to organize a great amount of content into a limited time, I carefully outlined my courses into general time periods, and then into units connected to historically significant events. The unit titles described the big ideas connected to these events. However, the course organization was based primarily on moving from one time period to another.

As I reviewed my units and events using the  framework, I realized that what I taught during the first half of the course was not necessarily informing and supporting what I taught during the second half. On reflection, I determined that time periods,

TOPIC: Modern United States History

Historical Themes

- The growth of participatory democracy
- The role of women
- Dissent and dissenters in American life
- Land use and the significance of the environment
- Religion in American History
- The role of ethnic and minority groups
- Work and the role of labor

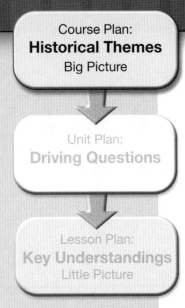

Course Plan:
Historical Themes
Big Picture

Unit Plan:
Driving Questions

Lesson Plan:
Key Understandings
Little Picture

which *are* useful organizers for the structure of a history course, *are not*, by themselves, historically meaningful or significant. Further, major events within each time period can be studied in many ways. As a consequence, historically significant connections between events in different time periods may not be as self-evident to students as they are to teachers. I needed to explore ways to tie together *what matters* over time for my students.

I began to look for the overarching themes that connected my units across major time periods. I needed to identify historically significant concepts, problems and types of events that appeared repeatedly across time periods. I asked myself:

- "What were the most significant changes in or characteristics of the United States over time?"

- "Which changes have been most enduring or part of a process that has unfolded across the stretch of time covered by my course?"

I looked for patterns embedded in my unit titles and reviewed national and state standards. I used the **TLH** historical categories of inquiry to check whether I was considering the full range of historical inquiry and experiences. I used my own skills and knowledge to decide that cultural and social history is as important to understanding American life as is political history. I determined to address historically significant ideas and events often given short shrift by traditional U.S. history programs.

This process led me to select seven historical themes: the growth of participatory democracy; the role of women; dissent and dissenters in American life; land use and the significance of the environment; religion in American history; the role of ethnic and minority groups; and work and the role of labor.

Understanding how Americans think about land, use it, and fight over it is central to understanding our nation. Land use patterns for much of the American colonial period through the late nineteenth century reveal a desire to shape the land for agricultural purposes or for wholesale extraction of natural resources. This often resulted in the devastation of native environments. By the progressive era, however, Americans began to think differently about both land and resources in ways that encouraged responsible use and conservation. Later in the 20th century, a fully developed conservation movement entered national life in the arenas of government, science, education, and private reform movements. Using this historical theme throughout the course allows students to consider why land and resource use have changed over time, and why that matters. This historical theme also promotes students' understanding of the historical literacy elements of *change and continuity, cause and effect and turning points*.

The same is true of the historical theme of work and the role of labor. This is a central characteristic of our national history so common that it often goes unseen in many history courses. For example, across units of American history I encourage students to use primary sources to explore how workers have viewed their work conditions, and how working people have responded, individually and collectively, to challenges posed by their work. This approach encourages students to see the past *through their eyes*, and helps them to *use the past* to understand how today's working conditions are shaped by those who came before.

It is important to choose themes that make sense to you, that matter historically, that are tied to national, state and local history standards, and that mesh with available materials and resources in your school setting. Keep them fresh and change them over time as your own historical knowledge grows. In the end, historical themes are vitally important because they give your course a coherent shape that students can recognize and use.

Unit Planning: Deciding What to Teach

I find myself trying to design unit lessons so students can <u>apply</u> material instead of memorization/ assessment only.

–TAH Teaching Fellow

State standards and district curricula identify far more information than students will understand and retain in any given year of study. Deciding which information is essential and which may be covered more lightly or not at all can be difficult. The **TLH** framework enables a teacher to narrow the instructional focus and determine an order of importance in choosing what to teach.

History begins with questions. A history unit begins with the development of driving questions. Driving questions serve as the bridge between the big picture historical themes identified for the course and the key understandings and learning goals for an individual lesson. One can begin by using the historical categories of inquiry and the historical themes for the course to identify the most significant aspects of the unit topic.

- Which events, people or ideas connected to this unit topic are most directly connected to the historical themes for the course?

    - See Getting Started: Finding Historical Themes, above, and the Resource section for references to sources that can help you do this.

- Are those connections *best demonstrated* or *historically significant* because they help one understand (one or more of the following):

    - Cause and effect?

    - Change and continuity?

    - Turning points?

    - Using the past?

    - Through their eyes?

Use your answers to these questions to decide what you will teach.

- Develop a limited number of declarative statements about what you want students to understand by the end of the unit. *"By the end of this unit students should understand _____"*

- Transform those declarative statements into questions. These become the driving questions for the unit. The driving questions should guide both teaching and student learning. Students should be able to answer the driving questions at the end of the unit.

The answers to the driving questions help students make sense of the content.

Look for ways to expose students to all of the historical categories of inquiry, as well as their accompanying pathway questions [See **TLH** Question Chart], as the year progresses. Look for ways to use these repeatedly so that students gain familiarity and facility using them to study the past.

COURSE PLAN: Historical Themes — Big Picture

Historically significant developments, types of activities or patterns that students can follow or pick up at multiple times during a school year and as they move from class to class.

The Historical Themes for this Course will be:

UNIT PLAN: Driving Questions

Bridge between historical themes (big picture, above) and key understandings (lesson, below) Promotes deep understanding of historically significant era or events. Focuses on the era or events in terms of historical categories of inquiry. Driving Questions inform lesson design and define what students should know at the end of the unit.

Unit Topic:	Unit Topic:	Unit Topic:	Additional Units...
Driving Question:	Driving Question:	Driving Question:	

[Excerpted from Curriculum Planning for History Worksheet, Resources section]

Course Plan:
Historical Themes
Big Picture

Unit Plan:
Driving Questions

Lesson Plan:
Key Understandings
Little Picture

• **The Built Environment: Middle School**

As I plan units for my middle school classes I need to pay attention to state standards and to all five strands of social studies (geography, history, political science, economics and behavioral sciences).

I do this by placing history at the center of my social studies curriculum. I have found that comprehension skills improve when students act as historical detectives and seek answers to driving questions. Students also gain a cogent understanding of the five strands of social studies as they learn to answer the driving questions. I use these tenets when planning eighth grade social studies units.

In this unit I wanted my students to explore the course themes related to the built environment. Since the unit was going to focus on the built environment I decided that this was a good opportunity to study something that my students could "feel and touch." Instead of studying the built environment in a place they had never been, we would learn history from the built environment in a place that mattered to them – their own community.

The course themes related to the built environment are connected to the historical categories of *change and continuity* and *using the past*. Studying the built environment in our local community would allow my students to discover that the past, historical change and evidence of change are part of their everyday world. The local connection would grab students' attention and the materials needed to teach the unit would be close at hand.

TOPIC: The Built Environment

Historical Themes: (partial list)

- The built environment is affected by the type of natural resources located in a region
- Archeological remains and architectural structures connect the people who lived in the past with the people who live in the present

Driving Questions:

- In what ways did the early residents of our community use natural resources to alter their environment?
- How does evidence from Beloit's archeological record and architectural structures demonstrate change?
- How does identifying historical architecture of the past help us make sense of our community today?

One of my course themes integrates history and geography strands by focusing on the relationship between natural resources and the man-made environment. Course theme: The built environment is affected by the type of natural resources located in a region. Combining this with the historical category of change and continuity can lead to an understanding of how each generation or group that lived in this area left evidence of its presence and its culture. I developed driving questions that would direct my students to this understanding: In what ways did the early residents of our community use natural resources to alter their environment? How does evidence from Beloit's archeological record and architectural structures demonstrate change?

Another course theme integrates the social studies strands by focusing on the ways that the built environment connects past and present. Course theme: Archeological remains and architectural structures connect the people who lived in the past with the people who live in the present. Combining this with the historical categories of change and continuity and using the past can lead to an understanding of why our city looks the way it does today. I developed a driving question that would direct my students to this understanding: How does identifying historical architecture of the past help us make sense of our community today?

Art Deco Strong Building in the Downtown District. Built c.1929

Queen Anne Style Home on Beloit's East Side. Built c.1905

Although I didn't have the answers to these driving questions when I began planning this unit, the course themes and driving questions helped me locate sources quite easily. The local library had information about historic buildings in our city. I obtained a glossary of architectural styles from the state historical society. I used

Course Plan:
Historical Themes
Big Picture

Unit Plan:
Driving Questions

Lesson Plan:
Key Understandings
Little Picture

these to identify significant architectural structures in the city of Beloit – structures from historical eras and groups we would study during the semester, structures that used different types of local resources, structures that are still standing and would be familiar to my students. Then, a colleague and I took pictures of these structures and buildings. I planned to use these to take my students on a virtual tour of the city.

The lessons that grew out of this unit were very successful. Excitement filled the room when students recognized public spaces, places of worship, museums, and neighborhoods. When they saw the effigy mounds students quickly realized that American Indians once inhabited the area where a college campus is now situated. They drew connections between local clays and the red and white brick that characterizes early government buildings and houses of worship. As the tour continued, students discovered that the local river once served as a dividing line between the west side, home to the area's first African Americans enticed by jobs and company-built housing during World War I, and the older established east side White community, reflected in architecturally distinct housing styles. Local building of many styles (Italianate, Queen Anne, and Art Deco) provided a timeline of the city's development in the late 19th and early 20th centuries.

TOPIC: *Progressive Era*

Historical Themes: (partial list)

- Society's attitudes about gender affected how people acted and the choices they made

Driving Questions:

- What effects did women and women's organizations have on social reform during the progressive era?

- Why did white women gain the right to vote in 1920?

• *Progressive Era: High School*

When I began planning this unit on the progressive era for my high school class I was overwhelmed by the number of people, ideas and events that could be "covered." My textbook chapter on the progressive era devotes more space than usual to discussing women. So, I decided that this would be a unit to focus on my course theme about gender attitudes and people's actions. Course theme: Society's attitudes about gender affected how people acted and the choices they made. I took out a pad of paper and began to organize my thoughts.

[this example is intended to be suggestive, not comprehensive]

People, Ideas, Events - - -

Settlement house movement, TR/New Nationalism vs WW/ New Freedom vs Debs/ Socialism, Triangle Shirtwaist Factory Fire, Jane Addams, Ida B. Wells, Samuel Gompers, trade unions, social gospel, juvenile justice reform, immigrant workers and neighborhoods, political reforms (16-19th amendments, initiative, referendum & recall, FDA & regulatory agencies, factory safety laws), NAACP, anti-lynching campaign

Connections between unit topic and historical theme:

• *Cause & Effect:* (1) Jane Addams and many women reformers did not marry. Instead they created a new kind of home and career for themselves in settlement houses. Through settlement work women reformers put their college education and concerns about women, children, democracy and justice to work for healthier and safer communities and workplaces (2) Ida B. Wells, like most African-American women, worked to support her family. More than most, she dedicated herself to work that combined earning income and serving the needs of her race; exposed economic motives for lynching and led a national movement against lynching

• *Change and Continuity:* (1) progressive era solutions to problems created by industrialization were pushed by women and focused on "feminine" concerns (family, children, health) (2) new roles for government and who could participate in government included a new definition of citizenship that included white women

By the end of this unit students should understand that:

• Women and women's organizations were very important in identifying what needed to be reformed and in promoting reform to solve problems caused by industrialization

• Women worked many years while facing significant opposition to earn the right to vote; it was not "given" to them.

Driving questions:
• In what ways did women and women's organizations participate in progressive era reform?

• How and why did white women gain the right to vote?

Lesson Planning – The Little picture

Thinking Like a Historian has helped me focus my lesson planning so I can defend the choices I make with credible evidence of pedagogy to the 'powers that be'.

–TAH Teaching Fellow

Lessons within a unit of study must have a clear instructional purpose. Lessons must focus on a key understanding as defined by the driving questions. In order to plan an effective history lesson a teacher needs to keep this completed statement in mind:

"By the end of this lesson I want my students to understand _____."

Teachers can use the historical process, as described by the **TLH** framework, to translate generic best practice lesson planning into effective history-specific lesson planning. Students need to use **TLH** skills and categories of inquiry in meaningful ways. Engaging and relevant activities create long-term understanding.

Lessons Components:	Effective History Lessons
Content Content is what a student should know, understand, and be able to do as a result of the lesson.	**Content** Determined by thoughtfully selected historical themes and driving questions Include all of the following: facts, ideas, concepts, **TLH** skills and categories of inquiry Make it possible for students to achieve a level 3 or 4 understanding on the **TLH** rubric in at least one historical category of inquiry [See **TLH** Rubrics in Sections 2 & 4]
Process Process is the instructional strategies designed to help the student understand the content.	**Process** Models the historical process (questions, evidence, interpretation) Engages students in inquiry and investigation of a historical "problem" (the historical problem is defined by the driving questions and key understandings) Uses multiple sources and different types of sources (including combinations of primary and secondary sources) Provides opportunities for students to use content to construct informed answers to the driving questions.
Application Application is how the student demonstrates what he/she knows, understands, and is able to do.	**Application** Guides student to conclusions that include historical interpretation and significance Makes it possible to determine student's proficiency at one or more **TLH** skills and categories of inquiry

COURSE PLAN: Historical Themes — Big Picture

Historically significant developments, types of activities or patterns that students can follow or pick up at multiple times during a school year and as they move from class to class.

The Historical Themes for this Course will be:

UNIT PLAN: Driving Questions

Bridge between historical themes (big picture, above) and key understandings (lesson, below) Promotes deep understanding of historically significant era or events. Focuses on the era or events in terms of historical categories of inquiry. Driving Questions inform lesson design and define what students should know at the end of the unit.

Unit Topic:	Unit Topic:	Unit Topic:	Additional Units...
Driving Question:	Driving Question:	Driving Question:	

LESSON PLAN: Key Understandings — Little Picture

Instructional purpose is determined by the historical themes for the course (big picture) and driving questions for the unit. Explains what students will understand at the end of the lesson. Includes Content, Process and Application.

Key Understandings:	Additional Lessons...	Additional Lessons...
Lesson Content:		
Lesson Process:		
Lesson Application:		

[Excerpted from Curriculum Planning for History Worksheet, Resources section]

Course Plan:
Historical Themes
Big Picture

Unit Plan:
Driving Questions

Lesson Plan:
Key Understandings
Little Picture

Examples from the Field *Lesson Planning*

- **Economic Change: From Farming to Industry, 1840s–1990s. Elementary School**

I want my fourth grade students to think like historians during each social studies lesson on state history. All my lessons on state history are grounded in two basic historical questions: *What has changed? How does the past help us make sense of the present?*

For this lesson I applied these questions to the changes in Wisconsin's economy, which moved from farming to manufacturing during the period under study. By the end of this unit I want my students to understand that:

- Agriculture evolved dramatically over the past 150 years, allowing farmers to grow far more food with far less labor. (This was much greater and rapid change than occurred over the preceding thousands of years.)

- Farming jobs dissolved with these agricultural improvements.

- Innovation resulted in industrialization.

- Manufacturing replaced agriculture as the primary source of income in Wisconsin as the Industrial Revolution came of age.

I planned this lesson to begin with a hook connected to what my students already know. They come to fourth grade knowing that agriculture requires fertile soil and a climate conducive to growing a variety of crops and livestock. I introduce the lesson by posing a question for my students:

"Our school is 157 years old. Until 50 years ago, every student who attended our school lived on a farm. Now none of you do. Why don't people live on farms in this community anymore?"

TOPIC: Economic Change: From Farming to Industry, 1840s–1990s

Historical Themes: (partial list)
- Economic changes are tied to existing natural resources as well as technological advances.

Driving Questions:
- What changed Wisconsin's workforce from primarily farmers to manufacturers?
- Why are fewer people farming than in the past and yet we still have enough to eat?

Key Understanding(s):
Students will understand that –
- new technologies in agriculture significantly increased the amount of food a farm can produce.
- the Industrial Revolution impacted Wisconsin's economy by shifting jobs from agriculture to manufacturing and increasing the urban population.

This leads to a class discussion about how farming evolved in Wisconsin from 1840 to the present. The purpose of this discussion is to develop questions that can help my students answer a variant of the hook question: Why do we have fewer farms and yet more people? We also contemplate what happened to all the farmers. This discussion produces a list of questions that, with a bit of editing, typically looks like this:

- What changes in agriculture occurred during this period?
- How did transportation change?
- What other ways did people make a living?
- Why did farms turn into subdivisions?
- How come we have enough food without all the farms?
- Were there any specific events that caused the reduction in farms?
- How has this decrease affected the state's economy?

The next step in the lesson, and in doing history, is to find information that will help to answer these questions. I provide a variety of historical sources and make sure that students understand that these are different types of sources and present different perspectives. I give students an opportunity to "digest" what they learn from each source through short writing assignments.

- <u>Secondary source account</u> of changes in farming technology provides details on new scientific and technological advances from the steel plow in the 1820s to crop rotation, fertilization, tractors, hybrid seeds and biotechnology; includes information on changes in the number of people a single farmer could feed per year[7]

  - Students write an analysis of the agricultural industry data

- <u>Oral history primary source</u> visit by an area farmer talks about the changes he's experienced in his 40 years of farming.

  - Students write a letter to the farmer. In addition to personal comments they must tell the farmer what they learned from his presentation.

[7] Wisconsin Agriculture Association, *This Business Called Agriculture*, (Wisconsin, 2007)

Course Plan:
Historical Themes
Big Picture

Unit Plan:
Driving Questions

Lesson Plan:
Key Understandings
Little Picture

- Secondary source biographies of leading inventors including Edison, Bell, Eastman, Ford, Deere and the Wright brothers allow students to see them as people.
  - Students prepare a biographical report that recognizes their inventor's innovation as a turning point and explains how it impacts our world today.
- Secondary source readings on the problems and conflicts that grew out of industrial development introduce students to more substantive studies.
  - Class discussion about poverty, child labor, organized labor, distribution of wealth, and the Wisconsin connection to the progressive movement.
  - Excellent challenges for interested and motivated students.

At this point we return to our initial set of questions. Students use the information and insights from their study of each source to answer that initial set of questions. The *process of thinking like historians gives them a better understanding of how Wisconsin shifted from agriculture to manufacturing.*

The lesson concludes with another brainstorming session that builds on what they have learned, connects this lesson to those that follow, and reminds students that historical events have long term consequences. The class develops questions concerning the long-term effects of this economic shift from a farming economy to a manufacturing economy. Their questions typically include:

- How have these changes affected our food supply?
- What do these changes mean to our environment?
- How have these changes affeted different groups in our society?

As a high school U.S. history teacher I was planning a lesson as part of a unit on the economic and social transformation of post-WWII America. Students will have spent several days examining social changes and how those changes affected various Americans. Focusing on the historical category of change and continuity, I decided to highlight the beat movement as an example of reaction to change, in particular a rejection of traditional values. This was also a good opportunity to collaborate with our language arts teachers who helped me and my students identify the literary characteristics of this kind of poetry.

I began the lesson by reading a poem from the beat movement. Students listed examples of social changes of the postwar period rejected by the poet. After this discussion, the class used a brainstorming activity to list other examples of postwar changes. Then students are asked to create a beat poem critical of the values represented by the postwar changes. Students are given an opportunity to share their poems with the class.

TOPIC: *Economic Change: Post-World War II America*

Historical Themes: (partial list)

- Reaction to change can be seen in cultural expressions

Driving Questions:

- How did the economic, cultural, and political changes of the post-war era affect different groups of Americans and American social life?

Key Understanding(s):
Students will understand that —

- members of the beat generation rejected the traditional values of 1950s mainstream culture and challenged conformity through writing, poetry, and art.

As a result of this lesson, I want my students to know and be able to identify examples of the social, economic, political, or cultural changes of postwar America (Change and Continuity) and to be able to explain different points of view (Through Their Eyes). The poem demonstrates students' ability to synthesize information and demonstrate written communication skills. Further, in addressing change and continuity, I can make connections to later developments of rock-n-roll, the counterculture, and to teenagers today. In this way, students have a deeper understanding of the nature of popular culture and the role social factors play in the construction of popular culture in a given time.

Making History Engaging AND Meaningful

The TLH skills have given me a concrete way to show how history is relevant and important to students' lives.

–TAH Teaching Fellow

Students engaged in constructing history are students engaged in learning history.

Many students believe that history is boring, full of facts, dates and rote memorization. Thinking Like a Historian changes that notion. **Rather than teaching students about history, TLH engages students in doing history.** It supports creative teaching that "hooks" students and draws them into the subject. When students are engaged in constructing history they become engaged in learning history. They want to learn more, rather than do the minimum needed to get by. When students are participants in their own learning, they are engaged and the material they are learning becomes much more meaningful to them.

A meaningful lesson is a lesson from which students learn in the short term AND remember that knowledge in the long term. How do we know if a lesson is engaging and meaningful to students? How can we distinguish between an engaging lesson that is meaningful and one that is just "fun"? The key to making history engaging and meaningful at the same time is to draw students into what they are studying and give them the skills to use this newfound knowledge. If students feel they are a part of the process they are more likely to take a vested interest in the outcome. This kind of lesson is:

- *Relevant to Students*
  Imagine learning about people born thousands of years before you, in a place you have never heard of, doing things that you don't care about. Would you be interested? If a history lesson can be made relevant to students, they are much more apt to become engaged in finding out more about the topic. We need to relate historical events to things that matter in our students' lives. This does not mean pretending that the past was exactly like the present or vice versa. Instead, teachers can make the past relevant, and model critical thinking by

  - highlighting big picture commonalities between past and present (international and domestic crises can lead to war, new technologies change relations between family and friends, societies make laws to achieve a vision of order and stability, belief systems affect individual and society-wide behaviors)

  - drawing connections between causes or consequences of a historical event and students' present day lives (roots of present day customs and beliefs, historic origins of everyday items, historical turning points that contributed to the opportunities or problems current in students' lives)

  - introducing a historical topic in terms of a problem, challenge or incomplete story to be investigated (partial or conflicting evidence about the causes or consequences of an event, stories about the actions or experiences of a real person)

• *Uses Primary Sources to Bring the Past Alive*
The best way to make history engaging and meaningful is to tell stories of the past using the words and pictures of those who lived it. Using primary source documents is an excellent way to draw students into history, into factual details and specific events as well as the emotions and choices that shaped those events. In doing so, teachers must be careful to choose sources that are authentic and that allow students to "see" the event or subject of study from multiple vantage points. Create research opportunities for students to participate in the search for these sources, to identify sources that are most meaningful to them, and to authenticate those sources and the stories that emerge from the sources.

• *Calls on Students to Apply their Knowledge*
In order to find history meaningful students need to be able to <u>do</u> something with the information they are learning. They need to be able to draw conclusions and educated inferences from the knowledge they are gaining, and to apply those concepts to their own lives and events happening around them.

Create lessons that ask students to participate in meaningful, relevant history. Lessons should lead to knowledge that students will be able to use in and out of the classroom. Avoid activities that use gimmicks simply to make history more "fun" for a day.

Course Plan:
Historical Themes
Big Picture

↓

Unit Plan:
Driving Questions

↓

Lesson Plan:
Key Understandings
Little Picture

Examples from the Field *Making History Engaging AND Meaningful*

- **War: Consequences of the U.S. Civil War. Elementary School**

Sometimes numbers *can* talk. They can remind us of powerful realities. This type of primary source information can bring the past alive. Take the following passages found in a *New York Times* book review:

> "The Civil War pitted brother against brother in the bloodiest conflict in American history. The North put 2.2 million men in uniform, half of its entire draft age population; the South mustered 800,000 men, an astounding 75 percent of its white draft-age population. More soldiers died -- about 625,000 -- than in all of America's 20th-century wars.
>
> *Some states took decades to recover. A third of Mississippi's 78,000 soldiers were killed in battle or died from disease. And more than half of the survivors brought home a lasting disability of war. Mississippi resembled a giant hospital ward, a land of missing arms and legs. In 1866, one-fifth of the state budget went for the purchase of artificial limbs."* [8]

You can paraphrase such passages for students and ask, what did those numbers *look like*? Small teams of fourth- and fifth-grade students can research pre-selected sites on the internet for both statistical and visual information for other states (or that information can be easily gathered and provided to them if time is of the essence).[9] They can graph this relatively simple statistical data. Their results can be discussed as a class, and then each student can write or present a response to the question about impact.

TOPIC: War: Consequences of the U.S. Civil War

Historical Themes: (partial list)
- Wars have Consequences
- Finding historical stories in the numbers

Driving Questions:
- What impact did the Civil War have on different states in the North?
- What impact did the Civil War have on different states in the South?
- What conclusions can you draw from the evidence?

Key Understanding(s):
Students will be able to –
- compare and contrast losses in individual states and between regions.
- construct interpretations of the impact of those losses by citing evidence.
- explain how war served as a turning point in the lives of those who participated and their families and communities.

[8] David Oshinsky, "Review: Web Sites with Civil War Lore Are as Popular as the Battlefields,"
New York Times, 2 November 2002,
http://query.nytimes.com/gst/fullpage.html?res=9E07E7DE1130F931A35752C1A9669C8B63
[9] State by state casualty statistics can be found at:
http://www.civil-war.net/searchstates.asp?searchstates=Total

Students become engaged as experts in a particular aspect of the war. Few adults share the kind of knowledge that they have uncovered. Most importantly, this is not historical trivia. The driving questions direct students to use the historical evidence they have uncovered to think about aspects of the post-war era that are often neglected. Rather than focusing study of the post-war era on the single issue of political reconstruction, this lesson prompts students to consider multiple consequences of war.

• War: The Holocaust as part of World War II. High School

In creating a unit on World War II, I knew that I wanted to cover the Holocaust in such a way that students in my U.S. history class would be able to understand the enormity of the event. I wanted my students to be able to see the Holocaust through the eyes of both those who perpetrated the Holocaust and those who were victims of the Holocaust. I also wanted them to be able to decipher the role of the Holocaust in WWII. *Through Their Eyes* from the Thinking Like A Historian chart helped me create a lesson that was engaging and meaningful without crossing the line into "imagined history."[10]

I used primary source material from the United States Holocaust Memorial Museum to create information packets about real people caught up in the Holocaust.[11] I purposefully created information packets for people who experienced the Holocaust in different ways, including "bystanders" (those who watched the Holocaust, but did nothing to stop it), victims, perpetrators, American soldiers, and resistance fighters.

TOPIC: War: The Holocaust as part of World War II

Historical Themes: (partial list)
- Wars have unintended and unanticipated consequences
- Wars have been significant turning points

Driving Questions:
- How were individual families and/or groups affected by the Holocaust?
- What role did different types/groups of people play in the Holocaust?
- How were they affected by it and how did they affect the event itself?

Key Understanding(s):
Students will understand that –
- the Holocaust involved many different groups of people (eg. socialists, Jews of different nationalities, government bureaucrats, businesses).
- different groups of people had different attitudes about and experiences of the Holocaust (victims, perpetrators, bystanders/collaborators).
- the Holocaust played a particular role in WWII and its <u>effects</u> as a turning point in history (eg. not a <u>cause</u> of the war; it changed the population of Europe, discredited racism, led to international laws forbidding crimes against humanity).

---

[10] See "Classroom Practice – Classroom Activities: What Works? Cautions and Pitfalls" for a discussion of Imagined History.
[11] United States Holocaust Memorial Museum, Washington D.C. http://www.ushmm.gov

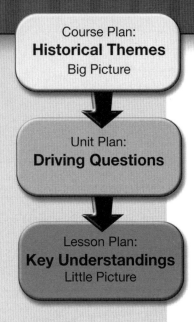

Course Plan:
Historical Themes
Big Picture

Unit Plan:
Driving Questions

Lesson Plan:
Key Understandings
Little Picture

At the beginning of the World War II unit I gave each student a badge with the name and photo of one of these people. Each day of the week students received more information about what was happening to that person as the war progressed. I asked students to write a daily journal *Through the Eyes* of the person they were following. Students had to use the information about what was happening to this person as the war progressed in combination with knowledge about the course of the war and the Holocaust, to reflect on how that person may have been experiencing his or her situation. On the last day, students learned whether that person had lived or died, and the circumstances surrounding his or her fate.

This activity made my students curious about the person they were following. It hooked them into learning more about the Holocaust and made them interested in detailed information about the history of the time. My students became more aware of the many different ways in which the Holocaust affected individuals and families. They learned to use that information to draw better conclusions about the time period as a whole.

This activity also asked students to look at the Holocaust from the viewpoints of different people, not just the victims. It helped my students draw their own conclusions about the relationship between individual actions and historical events. Had the person they followed merely been a pawn in history? Or, had he or she had an impact, no matter how small, on the course of events? It helped them relate the Holocaust to the larger struggles occurring during the war and engaged them in drawing their own cause and effect questions and answers. This helped to clear up misconceptions. Often students believe the Allies found the concentration camps, were horrified, and then fought harder to end the war. This exercise helped to show them that wasn't the case; the Holocaust was one event within the larger world war, and not a cause of war.

Contrast this hook with one where students are asked to simulate the concentration camp selection process. This is inconceivable and a-historical. While we can teach facts about and emotions generated by the Holocaust, we can never put ourselves in the shoes of someone who experienced or perpetrated such a horrific event. We cannot ask our students to become a historical figure and to act as that person would – for none of us has the worldview or particular experiences of a person from the past. Nor can such role playing ever have the life-threatening or life-altering implications that informed the real choices made by real people in the past. We can, however, give students first-hand accounts and allow them to see the past through the eyes of those who lived it, and to draw their own conclusions about how those figures affected and were affected by history.

EVALUATING PRE-EXISTING LESSONS

Thinking Like a Historian is not a new kind of history. It does not replace what many history teachers are already doing. Instead, **TLH** provides a model to enhance and improve instruction and learning. Teachers can use **TLH** to craft lessons that are more complete and historically accurate. Of course, it is not necessary to begin from scratch. **TLH** can be used as a tool to evaluate pre-existing lessons, both those that you have developed and those developed by publishers or other teachers.

> **"Another teacher told me about a great lesson on _____?
> It comes complete with resources, worksheets, activities, rubrics,
> everything. Should I use it?**

Good lessons focus on the driving question. The activities should respond to that question. The activities should not drive instruction or be an end in and of themselves. These questions can help you determine whether a lesson engages students in doing history and helps them make connections to significant historical themes, or if a lesson merely asks students to read and recite historical facts or to learn about disconnected events.

_____ How well is the lesson or activity connected to the essential understanding for the unit?

_____ How effectively does the lesson or activity promote students' ability to develop an answer to the driving questions?

_____ How effectively will the essential understandings be taught and learned?

_____ Will the lesson or activity help students develop a better understanding of one or more **TLH** historical process or category of inquiry?

_____ Does the lesson or activity allow the teacher to check for student understanding of those **TLH** processes and categories of inquiry? Consider both formative and summative assessment.

_____ Does the lesson or activity allow students to express or demonstrate their learning?

_____ Does the rubric used to assess student work accurately examine student learning in this lesson or activity? (The rubric should explicitly identify the content and **TLH** processes and categories that students are required to understand, know, and be able to do. Rubrics should not focus on behaviors or quantity of product.)

_____ Is the value to students in completing the lesson, activity or assessment proportional to the time it will take to complete it?

Teaching Tips:

Use the **TLH** Rubrics to evaluate individual assessments: Compare an existing assessment or textbook question to the **TLH** Rubrics. Does it score high on the rubric? If not, use the rubric as a guide to redesign the assessment. Redesigned questions should have a clear focus connected to one or more **TLH** elements of historical literacy. The quality of student performance improves as students have repeated opportunities to work with these elements and understand that these are learning goals. [See Instruction and Lesson Planning Rubric in Resource section]

Use the **TLH** categories of inquiry to evaluate course assessments: Collect all questions and assessments used during the semester into a single file. This can be done manually or digitally. Next to each write the element(s) of historical literacy that is most clearly addressed by that question or assessment. Then, consider the full picture. Over the course of the semester are students being asked to consider only one category of inquiry? For example, do all or most of the questions ask about cause and effect? Or, are students given practice and opportunities to examine the full range of historical categories, such as turning points and using the past? By incorporating **TLH** in course and unit planning one is better able to teach and assess all the **TLH** elements of historical literacy.

Course Plan:
Historical Themes
Big Picture

Unit Plan:
Driving Questions

Lesson Plan:
Key Understandings
Little Picture

 Examples from the Field *Evaluating Pre-Existing Lessons*

• *Slavery in the United States. Elementary School.*

When I introduce the topic of slavery to my fourth grade students, I know they have no understanding of what life was like for the enslaved. Our textbook summarizes slavery in two paragraphs suggesting the Underground Railroad was a viable means of escape for slaves in the Southern states. A writing assignment appears in the Teacher's Resource Package that reads as follows:

Imagine you are a slave on a plantation. You have decided to run away to freedom. Write a short story about one day on the Underground Railroad.

Is this an assignment I should give to my students? NO The problem with this activity is that it allows, even encourages, students to create their own picture or story about slavery. It does not require that they use real historical information or evidence. In fact, this would not be possible based on the limited coverage in the textbook. In the absence of real historical information students will draw ideas from their own experiences, experiences far removed from the mid-19th century system of American slavery. Students who complete this assignment may walk away with a false understanding of slavery, its hardships and the possibilities of escape – a false understanding that they invented to answer this question. When I asked my fourth grade students what they thought other fourth graders might write in response to this question one student suggested that the means of escape would be like the subway he once rode in Chicago.

TOPIC: Slavery in the United States

Historical Themes: (partial list)

• Slavery was a system of forced labor that benefited a limited class of people

• Few slaves were able to escape the system

Driving Questions:

• Why did slavery exist in this country?

• What was life like for the millions of people who were slaves?

Key Understanding(s):
Students will be able to understand that –

• Africans were kidnapped and sold into slavery in the Americas for over 200 years.

• the Underground Railroad is the euphemism for the slaves' practice of fleeing the southern slave states by walking north at night and occasionally hiding in abolitionists' homes by day.

• relatively few slaves succeeded in escaping the South and slavery until after the Civil War.

I decided to modify this pre-existing lesson activity by turning the question on its head. Rather than asking students to answer the question, the class brainstormed questions we would need to answer *before* we could "imagine" a response.

- What was being a slave like?
- Why would a slave want to escape?
- What was the Underground Railroad?
- Could anybody escape that way?
- Was escaping dangerous?
- Would other people be escaping, too?
- Where would an escaped slave go?
- Would an escaped slave know anyone?
- What if an escaped slave got caught?

This activity conjured questions, not answers. It taught my students that doing history means starting with questions. Finding out what we don't know starts with asking good questions, an essential skill for thinking like a historian.

Course Plan:
Historical Themes
Big Picture

↓

Unit Plan:
Driving Questions

↓

Lesson Plan:
Key Understandings
Little Picture

• **The First Industrial Revolution: Historical Simulation. Middle School.**

Pre-Existing Lesson:

During preparation for a unit on the first Industrial Revolution a metamorphosis in my thinking occurred. I noticed a problem in one portion of the unit, a candy factory simulation. For several years the students had worked on an assembly line to mass-produce identical candy boxes. Students were actively engaged in this simulation. In fact, a former student told me that she still has the candy box she produced. Yet, I realized that something was wrong. I asked myself: "Was it as authentic a representation of the First Industrial Revolution as it could be?" The answer was clearly no. Most obviously, this kind of learning activity should represent the production process or work experience of the first Industrial Revolution. The candy factory simulation did not do this. It did not help my students understand the specific characteristics of factory work in the early 19th century, before processed foods and assembly line production became common.

Adapting the Lesson:

I rethought and redesigned the unit and simulation using focus questions based on the  Question Chart. The Question Chart was used to craft topic-specific questions connected to my historical theme. In this case my broad historical theme was economic changes in production processes and work experiences. What purpose should or could a factory simulation serve? How could it help my students achieve the key understandings for the lesson?

My students are thirteen and fourteen years old, ages similar to the children who worked in the Rhode Island and Lowell system mills. During the unit on the first Industrial Revolution we read a play about the "Lowell Mill Girls" in an issue of *Junior Scholastic*. Students read about the harsh conditions endured by the mill workers. Yet, I wondered if my students really understood the descriptions they read about child labor in the 19th century. I decided that a better factory simulation could help them to do this.

TOPIC: The First Industrial Revolution: Historical Simulation

Historical Themes: (partial list)
- Economic changes in production processes and work experiences

Driving Questions:
- How did economic changes during the first Industrial Revolution affect child workers and their communities?
- How have people understood, remembered or mythologized economic development?

Key Understanding(s):
Students will be able to understand –
- that factory production contributed to the change from an agricultural economy to a nation of wage earners living in cities.
- the conditions that made textile mill work difficult for child workers.
- the reasons some workers went on strike (called turnouts).

The factory simulation needed to focus on an early 19th century product – making cloth, not assembling candy boxes. The factory simulation needed elements that represented significant aspects of textile mill work. Of course, many aspects of early industrial factory work *cannot be simulated*. I thought carefully about which *could be simulated*.

Could be simulated	Cannot be simulated
The product: cloth	**Nature of work:** dangerous
Nature of work: highly repetitive	**Nature of work:** long workdays (up to 12 hours)
Nature of work: monotonous – uniformity required, individual creativity not permitted	**Work conditions:** massive machinery
Work conditions: strict work rules controlled personal behavior and earnings	**Work conditions:** noisy machinery
Workers attitudes and expectations: first-time experience of this kind of work	**Workers attitudes and expectations:** long-term experience of this kind of work

The redesigned simulation was much different from the original. I assigned specific work roles to each student (thread making, weaving machine tending, materials delivery, overseer). Desks were renamed work stations. Thread makers cut strips of construction paper, delivery workers carried these to work stations as requested by raised hands, machine tenders worked in pairs to weave construction paper threads according to a pre-assigned pattern, overseers checked the quality of the "woven cloth," enforced work rules, and reported violations to the factory superintendent (teacher). Factory rules, adapted from real factory rules from the Hamilton Manufacturing Company, 1848, were posted on the board.[13] We discovered that a class of twenty-five "workers" can produce approximately fifteen pieces of construction paper cloth by the end of a fifty-four minute period.

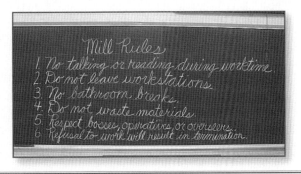

---

[13] Factory Rules from the *Handbook to Lowell*, 1848. http://www.kentlaw.edu/ilhs/lowell.html. [accessed 6/29/07].

Course Plan:
Historical Themes
Big Picture

Unit Plan:
Driving Questions

Lesson Plan:
Key Understandings
Little Picture

More importantly, the simulation helped my students understand essential elements of child labor during the first Industrial Revolution. How do I know that the students had a better understanding of what it might have been like to work in a factory during the first Industrial Revolution? At the end of the simulation, students wrote about their "work" experience. The next day they read their responses orally.

Student Responses	Teacher Reflection on Evidence of Student Learning
"I felt like I was a robot. Like I was programmed to do every thing and got turned on every day and then turned off every night. —Stephanie	This student recognized that mill workers had to work at a pace and doing tasks set by others, not by themselves (different from what would have been common on the 19th century family farm and different from her own 21st century life) 👀
"I think the children felt like I did, very closed in and almost not American. I felt as if I had no rights and that I should have been able to speak...go to the bathroom..." —Tesia	When Lowell workers turned out (went on strike) in the 1830s they claimed that their bosses were not respecting the rights that their ancestors had fought for in the Revolution. This is a good insight. Yet, this student presumes she is just like 19th century children. 👀
"It made me feel all the more sorry for anyone who had to really go through the experience. We were all at a comfortable temperature... our overseers weren't really that cruel. We didn't have long hours, and some people took it as a joke. If it had been real, we would have been in hot temperatures, had cruel overseers, had excruciatingly long hours, and if we had been fired, we would have been put on the "bad list". This was a list of workers that factories wouldn't hire because they stirred up trouble..." —Rachel	This student clearly understands that the classroom simulation was not the same as the real experience. Her explanations of the differences include details that reveal her understanding of the real work conditions and concerns of mill workers in the early 19th century. She does not discuss any rewards that workers gained from this work. 👀

Clearly, the simulation shaped their thinking about child labor on a political, economic and social level. Asking good historical questions and uncovering primary source documents appropriate for the period surveyed are essential components of **TLH**. Assessing students' knowledge after teaching the lesson requires reflective thinking from the student as well as the teacher. This is the reason I keep one foot planted in the past while casting one eye to the future. It keeps me focused-- Thinking Like A Historian.

Selecting Sources for the Classroom

I now incorporate primary documents into each unit I teach. This makes history come alive for my students.

–TAH Teaching Fellow

There are two types of historical sources. Each type of source fulfills a different purpose. Both are essential to history education.

Primary Sources are the building blocks of history. Primary sources are sources created at the time an event occurred or by people who were there when the event occurred. Letters, public speeches, newspaper articles, census reports, court records, private diaries, photographs, songs, e-mail messages, birth records, legislative debates and oral accounts are all primary sources.

- *Using primary sources* facilitates student understanding of the historical process, connects students directly to people and events in the past, and enhances student appreciation for the past.

Secondary Sources are interpretive accounts made after the historical event has passed. Authors of secondary sources rely on primary sources and other secondary sources for their information about the event. Journal or magazine articles, books, textbooks, maps, movies, documentaries, museum exhibits and living history re-enactments are all secondary sources.

- *Using secondary sources* provides students with the historical context needed to make sense of the primary sources, ensures that students have access to different historical interpretations, and ensures that students can find important information not included in necessarily limited sets of primary sources.

Finding primary and secondary sources for the classroom can be a problem in two ways. The first is simply finding materials on a given historical topic that are relevant and developmentally appropriate for students. As teachers we often need to find materials to better inform ourselves about unfamiliar topics. The Resource Lists in Section 4 offer a starting point.

> Finding Sources:
> Are they relevant and developmentally appropriate?

A second problem that can be overlooked as we search for anything "relevant" and "appropriate" has to do with the value and quality of the materials as historical sources for the specific lesson we are planning. Whether we are using sources already on hand or finding new sources, we should always stop to ask:

- Are these good historical sources?

- Will they provide the perspectives and information needed?

> Finding Sources:
> Will they support the specific lesson objectives?

ARE THESE GOOD HISTORICAL SOURCES?

Primary and Secondary Sources should be checked for both quality and validity. This is especially important for on-line or digitized sources. "Credentialing" historical sources is an important part of the historians' task. It is also an important research skill that should be taught in the history classroom. Credentialing a historical source means checking the "source of the source."

Who or what organization makes the source available to you?	Why has that person, organization or institution made the source available	Could this purpose introduce any bias or inaccuracies or special qualities into the sources that are made available?
Government agency	Education?	some pre-selection and/or editing of sources may have been made (this could be beneficial for teaching purposes)
	Advocacy?	may provide significant perspective; however, must consider bias inherent in purposeful intent to advocate
	Public Record?	may be very comprehensive for information provided; public charge defines/limits the type and classifications of information recorded
	Repository/Archive?	may be very comprehensive or quite limited depending on original creator/owner of the materials archived
Non-governmental organization • **Political** • **Trade (business)** • **Public service** • **Issue-specific reform**	Education? Advocacy? Self-promotion? Fund-raising? Recruitment/Membership?	may provide significant perspectives and may be the only or best source of information on certain topics must consider bias or accuracy inherent in purposeful intent to educate, advocate, self-promote, fund raise and/or recruit
Publishing house or film producer	Profit-making?	may provide significant perspectives or may ignore or "massage" significant perspectives or information to entice consumers (national or regional trade book publishers, movie producers)
	Education (K–12, university)?	some pre-selection and/or editing of sources may have been made (could be beneficial); may ignore significant perspectives or information due to pressures from educational agencies or advocacy groups (educational publishers, university or historical society presses, documentary film-makers)
	General public readers/viewers?	may not provide depth of information or range of perspectives needed to develop or support historical interpretations (local & self-published as well as national or regional book publishers)
Individual • **Oral history interview** • **Letters, photos, artifacts**	Education? Public Service? Professional or job duty? Self-promotion?	may provide a significant perspective must consider bias or accuracy inherent in purpose AND inherent in sharing memories influenced by passage of time and self-identity

Millions of wonderful and less-than-wonderful sources are readily available at the touch of our fingers through the **World Wide web**. Web-based sources must be credentialed like other sources. Teaching students to credential web-based sources is a particularly important skill. Attention to this skill is essential to developing proficiency at the historical process of gathering and evaluating evidence. It is a skill that students can and should transfer to all web-based research.

Sourcing web-based sources is quite similar to sourcing any other source. The chart above can serve as a guide for both. Teachers may also want to use the **Website Evaluation Worksheet** in the Resource section.

WILL THE SOURCES PROVIDE THE PERSPECTIVES AND INFORMATION NEEDED?

Good history teaching and learning require analysis of multiple sources. A single source, whether its a textbook narrative or a primary document, limits students to the author's explanation. Students cannot fully engage in historical inquiry and analysis based on a single source.

At the same time, providing multiple perspectives does not mean providing equal numbers of documents from two sides of an issue. This kind of "balance" does not necessarily lead to good historical understanding. It does not respect the historical process of evaluating and weighing all the relevant evidence. It does not allow consideration of different types of sources. It does not take into consideration the historical context of the event under study.

Choosing sources for the classroom is similar to what historians do when they prepare the end product of their research for publication or exhibit. By this point the historian has completed the research, evaluated and analyzed the evidence and reached a historical conclusion. The task at hand is to draw supporting and explanatory evidence from the full historical record.

Choosing sources for the classroom differs from this process in two noteworthy ways. First, there is neither time nor ability to study or take into consideration the "full historical record." The quantity and nature of the historical sources we use in the classroom must be selected with these practical constraints in mind. Second, K–12 history teaching is more tightly connected to specific learning objectives than is the historian's study of a particular topic. The historian can engage in open-ended inquiry that can lead down unexpected paths, some of which may be dead-ends. Certainly the sources we choose for our lessons should permit some degree of open-ended inquiry. However, those sources must be carefully selected to ensure that students can arrive at historically valid and supportable conclusions.

If students approach history as a discipline – a way of thinking – and not just a collection of facts arranged chronologically, then they must analyze primary sources. However, teachers must select those sources carefully. Several questions should guide this selection process, including:

_____ What do I want the document to "do" in the context of the lesson? How does the document relate to the key understandings or driving questions?

_____ Is the document accessible for students, and does it have value and use in relation to the time invested by the student?

_____ Does the document inform or speak to other materials, either primary or secondary, within the current unit?

_____ Does the document reinforce or connect with past learning, or does it foreshadow coming material?

_____ Does the document, because of its nature, reinforce the learning of a particular skill essential to historical literacy?

_____ Does the document's content challenge routinely held assumptions about a particular historical time period and its standard interpretation?

Will the sources I'm considering provide information, perspectives and ideas **directly relevant** to answering the driving questions?

If Yes: these may be good sources

Do the sources I'm considering provide information, perspectives and ideas **related** to the topic, but **not directly relevant** to answering the driving questions?

If Yes: these may not be good or sufficient sources

▶ **The driving question asks about the impact of early 19ᵗʰ century Indian Removal policy in the United States.**

The sources provide information about the populations, economies, politics and/or culture of Indian nations both before and after removal.

Reasons these may be good sources: In order to assess "impact" we must be able to compare the situation after an event to the situation before the event AND be able to connect any post-event changes to the event itself. Any given event will impact different groups of people, places and institutions in different ways. Thus, "impact" questions, and sources for answering those questions, may need to identify specific people, places or institutions in order to be manageable.

▶ **The driving question asks about the impact of early 19ᵗʰ century Indian Removal policy in the United States.**

The sources provide information about the Indian Removal Act and treaties signed with Indian nations in the 1830s.

Reasons these may not be good sources: The Removal Act and treaties are statements of policy and intent. They may offer some clues about the situation before, or leading up to those policy statements. They cannot provide information about impact, or what happened after they were implemented.

▶ **The driving question asks about the immigrant experience in the United States.**

The sources provide information about the kinds of jobs people held, the neighborhoods where they lived, the size of families, school experiences, and/or the organizations to which immigrants belonged.

Reasons these may be good sources: The question focuses on the lives of people once they are in the United States. The types of sources identified above can provide information about important elements of the human experience – the way people provided for basic human needs of food, shelter and clothing (jobs); the places people lived and who they lived with (neighborhoods and families); and social and cultural practices (schools and organizations).

▶ **The driving question asks about the immigrant experience in the United States.**

The sources provide information about traveling to the United States and/or about anti-immigrant politics and organizations.

Reasons these may not be good sources: The trip to the United States and anti-immigrant politics are both limited sub-sets of the immigrant experience. In the larger scope of an immigrant's life span traveling to the United States was of very short duration. Knowing details of that trip does not tell us anything about what that person experienced after they arrived. Sources related to anti-immigrant politics and organization can lead to a deeper understanding of the social climate that confronted immigrants in the "receiving society." This kind of information cannot tell us about a wide range of other factors pertinent to the immigrant experience (how they worked, lived, played, learned, met personal and national crises).

Do the documents I'm considering provide information, perspectives and ideas that will allow my students to reach **historically accurate** conclusions? *If Yes: these <u>may</u> be good sources*	Do the documents I'm considering provide information, perspectives and ideas that could lead my students to **historically incorrect** conclusions? *If Yes: these <u>may not</u> be good or sufficient sources*
▶ **The driving question asks about the arguments for and against women's suffrage.** The sources provide 2–3 pro- and 2–3 anti-suffrage perspectives: from the same time periods in which the authors use a range of economic, biblical, political and cultural arguments. *Reasons these may be good sources: This range of sources makes it possible to examine the multiple ideas and beliefs that motivated both groups. Using sources from the same time period ensures that the sources capture the debate and conflicts that actually occurred in the past.*	▶ **The driving question asks about the arguments for and against women's suffrage.** The sources provide a pro- and an anti-suffrage perspective: the 1848 Seneca Falls Declaration and an anti-suffrage speech by a U.S. Senator in 1918. *Reasons these may not be good sources: The United States changed enormously during the 70-year struggle for women's suffrage (1848–1919). Although some pro- and anti-suffrage arguments remained the same throughout that period, others did not. Using only two sources makes it extremely difficult to understand that real people took a stand on one or the other side of this struggle for a variety of reasons and that some ideas resonated more strongly than others at different points in time. Also, these documents were intended to accomplish very different purposes, which may have influenced the information and arguments that the authors included in these statements. The Seneca Falls Declaration was written to educate the general public and as a call to political action by a small, largely unorganized gathering of private citizens. The Senator's speech was intended as a statement of personal belief and/or to sway the vote of fellow Senators in the midst of a Congressional debate on a constitutional amendment.*
▶ **The driving question asks about the causes of World War II.** The sources provide information about political and economic crises and consequences of the 1930s economic depression and about national and international conflicts and instability arising from the WWI settlements in Asia, Europe and the United States. *Reasons these may be good sources: This choice of sources recognizes that the conflicts that erupted into World War II were directly related to the frustrations and measurable problems arising from two preceding events – World War I settlements and the economic depression of the 1930s. This range of sources can offer information on the regional wars in Asia and Europe that merged into a World War by the end of 1942.*	▶ **The driving question asks about the causes of World War II.** The sources provide information about Pearl Harbor and the Holocaust. *Reasons these may not be good sources: These sources would lead to an inaccurate understanding of when the war started and why the United States entered the war. Although the Japanese attack at Pearl Harbor was the proximate cause of United States entry into the war, the regional wars that would merge into WWII began a decade earlier. Although the horrors of the Holocaust were known to top government leaders on the Allied side during the war, they purposefully did not publicize this information, did not use it to promote or motivate their people to fight and explicitly refused to pursue military action targeting the death camp system.*

Course Plan:
Historical Themes
Big Picture

⬇

Unit Plan:
Driving Questions

⬇

Lesson Plan:
Key Understandings
Little Picture

Examples from the Field   *Selecting Sources for the Classroom*

 • *Immigration Nation. Elementary School.*

When I have my class research the impact of immigration on the United States from the Irish Famine of the 1840s through the present, I use a variety of primary and secondary sources. I have been careful to select sources that will help my students answer the driving questions and develop key understandings. There are many published fictional accounts about coming to this country. I avoid these, but I do use a number of first-person narrative accounts where the authors write of their own experiences as immigrants, but use fictional names for their characters.

As I prepared the lesson I considered what information and perspectives need to be embedded in the sources in order for my students to answer the driving questions and develop the key understandings. I used this list to figure out whether my sources are adequate for the lesson or not. This unit's success depends on the students having appropriate reading materials. My goal is to gather as wide a variety of primary and secondary sources, both easy reading and more challenging reading, that are credible and instructive. With the list in mind I began looking for sources. I checked:

- Library of Congress: This is a well-credentialed source with many easily accessible photographs, broadsides, drawings and political cartoons.

- Biographies, autobiographies and first person historical narratives about immigrants and migrants in my resource room and school library

TOPIC: Immigration Nation, 1840–present

Historical Themes: (partial list)

- Exploration, trade and immigration influenced change
- Peoples of three continents met both through voluntary and forced migration
- Immigrants were subject to "Push-Pull" factors

Driving Questions:

- What caused people to immigrate to this country during different time periods?
- What effects has immigration had on this country?

Key Understanding(s):
Students will understand that –

- immigration and forced migration brought millions of people from around the world to this country creating a diverse ethnic and racial population.
- immigrants left their homelands for many reasons (escaping from tyranny, overpopulation and poverty).
- immigrants settled on lands once occupied by Native people who were forced to relocate.
- immigrants brought customs, skills and talents that have contributed to this country's culture and economy.

- Local Resources – especially a nearby living history museum that recreates mid-19th century farmsteads representing Wisconsin's many European immigrant groups as well as a small Black migrant community.

- Class textbook.

The sources needed to help students find out: [example of my list in progress –later sorted and used by appropriate time period]

- **Who immigrated?**
  Pictures: family of immigrants looking at the Statue of Liberty as they arrive in New York harbor, immigrants on an Atlantic ocean liner, c. 1900, sketch of Africans on a slave ship
  1st Prsn Narr: Bette Bao Lord, *In the Year of the Boar and Jackie Robinson*
  Biographies: Allen Say, *Grandfather's Journey*, Alexander Graham Bell, Gloria Estafan. . .

- **Where did the immigrants come from? And When?**
  Lecture: numbers, national origins of immigrants, eras of high immigration
  Textbook: numbers, national origins of immigrants, eras of high immigration

- **What were the conditions in their home country at the time they immigrated?**
  1st Prsn Narr: Bette Bao Lord, *In the Year of the Boar and Jackie Robinson*
  Biographies: Allen Say, *Grandfather's Journey*, Alexander Graham Bell, Gloria Estafan. . .

- **What were the conditions in America at the time they immigrated?**
  Ads: 1800's advertisement of land for sale in Iowa and Nebraska called "Million of Acres"
  Lecture: Native American removal

- **What were the immigrants' customs and skills?**
  1st Prsn Narr: Bette Bao Lord, In the Year of the Boar and Jackie Robinson
  Biographies: Allen Say, Grandfather's Journey, Alexander Graham Bell, Gloria Estafan. . .

- **Where did immigrants settle in America? Why did they settle in those places?**

- **What happened to the communities, peoples or lands where the immigrants settled?**
  Lecture: Native American removal

- **What kinds of home, family, community and work lives did immigrants have?**

- **How did native-born Americans react to immigrants?**
  Political Cartoons: armed settler telling a Native American to "Go West"
  Non-Fiction: Ellen Levine, *If Your Name Was Changed At Ellis Island*
  1st Prsn Narr: Bette Bao Lord, *In the Year of the Boar and Jackie Robinson*

Course Plan:
Historical Themes
Big Picture

Unit Plan:
Driving Questions

Lesson Plan:
Key Understandings
Little Picture

• **Immigration & Westward Expansion, early 19ᵗʰ century. Middle School.**

I was preparing a unit on Westward Expansion and War, 1790–1860, for my 8ᵗʰ grade American History class. I developed driving questions for this unit connected to the historical theme of immigration, motives and policies. The driving questions focused on expansion into Mexican Texas as an example of immigration. The most common immigration stories place the United States as the receiving society. This topic offered a unique opportunity to think about Mexico as the receiving society. The driving questions were: What policies did the Mexican government set for Euro-Americans immigrating to Mexico in the 1820s? and How might those policies from the 1820s help us make sense of present day immigration?

TOPIC: Immigration & Westward Expansion, early 19ᵗʰ century

Historical Themes: (partial list)

• Immigration, motives and policies

Driving Questions:

• What policies did the Mexican government set for Euro-Americans immigrating to Mexico in the 1820s?

• How might those policies from the 1820s help us make sense of present day immigration?

Key Understanding(s):
Students will be able to –

• identify the requirements set by the Mexican government for Euro-American settlement in Mexican Texas.

• describe the kinds of citizens Mexico wanted the new immigrants to become.

• compare/contrast those immigration requirements to present day U.S. immigration requirements.

When I reviewed the textbook I discovered that it devoted less than one page to Euro-Americans in Texas. My students needed more background knowledge in order to answer these driving questions and make connections to the larger thematic focus on immigration. I decided to look for primary sources that could build their knowledge base.

I wanted primary sources because my students often think of historical events in a vacuum. For example, in class discussions students reported that they have Italian or German ancestry. However, when asked when their ancestors immigrated, they could only distinguish two points in time: those who were "born in Wisconsin" (themselves and their parents) and those who were born in Italy or Germany (any ancestor before their parents' generation). The historical timeline for past and present immigration was blurred.

My research for a document began with the *Magazine of History* published by the Organization of American Historians. I discovered an issue devoted to the subject of the American West. It contained an essay that examined Euro-American settlement in northern Mexico. The essay contained several gems for teachers, including historical background information, primary documents, and a teaching guide with discussion questions.

One of the primary documents fit my needs perfectly. It was a copy of the 1825 contract between Stephen Austin and the Mexican government that authorized Austin to settle 500 families in the Mexican state of Texas. The contract between Austin and the Mexican government contained strict conditions for Anglo and European immigration.[14] This document would make it possible for my students to read the actual contract provisions themselves. They could use these details to build their own understanding of the immigration goals and policies of the Mexican government. The document also allowed my students to "use the past" to better understand immigration today. Students could use this information to answer the driving questions. In addition, the *Magazine of History* essay contained copies of both the original handwritten contract and a typed transcript of the contract. Trying to read the handwritten document allowed my student to learn even more about differences between past and present.

Locating primary source material reminds me of searching for a lost item. It is exhilarating when the item is found, disappointing when it is not. Knowing where to look for primary source material can save teachers time and frustration. If an individual wants a new home, he might start with a local builder, contractor, or real estate agent. Similarly, when researching for primary source material of a historical nature, a logical place to start is with a historian or historical journal.

[14] "Transcript of Second Colony Contract Authorizing Stephen F. Austin to Settle 500 Catholic Families in the State of Cuahuila and Texas, June 4, 1825." Sam W. Haynes, "Teaching American History With Documents from the Gilder Lehrman Collection," in Organization of American Historians, *Magazine of History*, November 2005. According to the article, Gilder Lehrman has over 60,000 documents chronicling American history. Some of these are available on-line at the Gilder Lehrman Institute.

Course Plan:
Historical Themes
Big Picture

↓

Unit Plan:
Driving Questions

↓

Lesson Plan:
Key Understandings
Little Picture

• *World War I. High School.*

As I developed this lesson for my high school U.S. history course I wanted students to understand how World War I affected people in their daily lives. Although the textbook has some information, it's very general. I didn't think that my students understood that the textbook covered only part of the home front story and I didn't think that my students thought of the people in the textbook as "real people."

I decided to look for primary sources that would allow my students to explore the home front in their local community. Using a good primary source set would:

- help students understand the effects of the war *through the eyes* of people on the home front.

- be a nice hook to create interest in the effects of a long-ago war.

- make it possible to extend students' understanding by comparing the textbook account of the effects of war on the home front with the experiences of people in their community.

- give students practice using  skills: asking questions, evaluating sources, and developing interpretations

TOPIC: *World War I*

Historical Themes: (partial list)

- Home front during times of war

Driving Questions:

- What were the social, political, economic, and cultural changes in the United states during World War I?

Key Understanding(s):
Students will be able to –

- analyze newspapers as a primary source.

- interpret primary source newspapers to determine the effects of World War I on their community.

I chose to use local newspapers as the primary source. Although editorial and journalistic practices mean that newspapers are not full accounts of the home front, they can be very good sources. Local newspapers in the early 20th century carried detailed descriptions of local activities, events and people. The reading level is accessible to my high school students. Newspapers are readily available. Usually the local library or historical society has copies of old newspapers.

I found a microfiche copy of our local paper at the Wisconsin Historical Society. I skimmed various issues published during the time the United States was involved. I made copies of several news articles, advertisements, and pictures from the war era that illustrated effects of war in the community. It was exciting to read the paper myself. My students were surprised to discover an article that criticized the "most enthusiastic parents" for thinking that their own children should be exempt from going to war. They were intrigued by another article that accused five local people of being unpatriotic after they had been seen driving their cars in a neighboring town on a Sunday (the Fuel Administration had asked people to conserve fuel by not driving on Sundays).

CLASSROOM PRACTICE

Classroom Activities: What Works? Cautions and Pitfalls

The human imagination is the most powerful entity on Earth since it can transcend both time and space.
—Albert Einstein

As history teachers, our goal is to provide engaging classroom experiences that promote historical literacy, that is, inquiry and analysis of the past using primary and secondary sources. Since students naturally conjure images and "see" historical events, we need to exercise caution in choosing activities to illustrate the past. Simulating an 1853 dinner table conversation about the Fugitive Slave Act can promote student understanding. Simulating the Middle Passage from Africa to the Americas for an hour can distort student understanding. Debating the British and French decision to acquiesce to Germany's invasion of Czechoslovakia in 1938 can promote student understanding. Simulating the selection of Holocaust victims during 7th period can distort student understanding.

What is the difference between these related activities? At their best the dinner table conversation and the debate of British and French policy call on students to use historical knowledge, derived from secondary and primary sources, to reconstruct the attitudes and ideas real people would have held at the time. They call on students to consider the multiple factors (economic, political, social, religious, military) that shaped the worlds of 1853 and 1938. These activities call forth **historical imagination**.

In contrast, the Middle Passage and Holocaust simulations ask students to imagine that a simulation is the real thing. These activities position the simulation as a source of historical information, rather than using the simulation as a means to express or explore historical knowledge. These activities can lead to **imagined history**, filled with misconceptions about the past.

- Informed activities that respect the difference between past and present nurture the **historical imagination** of the learner.

- Contrived activities intended to develop empathy for the plight of people in the past can provide a false understanding or what may be characterized as **imagined history**.

The following chart contrasts classroom activities that nurture **historical imagination** with classroom activities that promote **imagined history**.

Classroom Activity
Debates

Students assigned to argue for or against a historical decision or action.

Historical Imagination How it Can Work	Imagined History Cautions & Pitfalls
• Can promote independent or guided research • Can foster understanding that the course of events is rarely "inevitable" or "obvious" • Can engage students in real historical ideas, choices, personalities and struggles.	• Focuses attention and places importance on the outcome of the class debate rather than the real historical events and their consequences • Incorrectly presumes that the class answer or winner is the same as historical understanding • Often allows students to substitute their own values, worldviews, personalities, historical beliefs for those of people in the past • In the interest of time or engagement often ignores significant historical factors such as context, personalities, multiple perspectives, differences in power, authority and knowledge, real historical events.
▶ **Example:** **Was President Truman's decision to drop two atomic bombs consistent with or a departure from American wartime ideals, goals and tactics?**	▶ **Example:** **Should the Atomic Bomb have been dropped?**
Posed in this manner, the debate question focuses research and discussion on the real historical actors and the arguments and positions that real people took in the context of the world they lived in at the time.	Posed in this manner, the debate question does not specify any standard by which students should evaluate the decision to drop the bomb. In fact, the wording of this question inclines students to use their own ethics or "presentism" in place of understanding the decision to drop the atomic bomb as a historical event: The question makes no reference to the real historical situation in 1945, the factors that decision-makers could have or would have been expected to take into consideration at that time, or the limited numbers of people who had the power to influence or make this decision.

Classroom Activity
Editorials

"Write an editorial about _____."

Historical Imagination How it Can Work	Imagined History Cautions & Pitfalls
• Can promote understanding that people in the past disagreed about the best course of action • Can promote understanding that there were multiple sides or perspectives on an issue or event and that these often reflected an individual's particular position in society (class, gender, race/ethnicity, region, religion….) • Can promote an understanding of the large thematic ideas or issues surrounding a specific event or struggle.	• Can easily fall into "presentism," using one's own worldview, ethics or motives to support the editorial position. In contrast, historical understanding means understanding the worldview, ethics and motives of people in the past. • Editorials are a form of persuasive communication that purposefully uses some information or ideas and ignores other information or ideas. This genre of communication makes it difficult to use specific historical evidence (as opposed to broad themes) and to explain cause and effect or change and continuity. • Can reward students for passion and engagement over depth of historical understanding and mastery of information
▶ **Example:** **You are a member of the Red Guard during the Cultural Revolution in China. Write a letter to the editor of your local paper explaining why you joined the Red Guard and why people should obey the Red Guard.**	▶ **Example:** **You are living in Beijing, China during the Cultural Revolution. Write an editorial explaining your support for or your opposition to the Red Guard.**
Posed in this way the editorial prompts students to set aside their own worldview and to speak with the voice of a young Chinese man or woman active in the Cultural Revolution. The prompt encourages students to consider multiple reasons young people flocked to the Red Guard. The prompt encourages students to explore the ways in which Red Guard defined their own mission and achievements, as opposed to the ways in which the Chinese Communist Party leadership used the Red Guard. In this respect, the editorial can enhance a deeper exploration of the differences between individuals who enact state policy on the ground and the goals or motives of political leaders and state policy.	Posed in this way the editorial allows students to use their own worldview. Students are not prompted to delve into the real experiences, values and concerns of Chinese during the Cultural Revolution or to recognize that attitudes were highly dependent on age, education, class and political affiliation. The prompt does not require students to connect opinion about the Red Guard to these crucial characteristics. While student choice and examining two sides of an issue are sound practices, it is difficult to use the editorial format to achieve this goal for this type of event. In fact, such an editorial prompt could result in historical misunderstanding by leading students to the incorrect conclusion that there was open public debate during this era. There was not. Opponents of the Cultural Revolution or the Red Guard risked their lives, even when they used carefully coded language.

Classroom Activity
Hooks
Lesson openers designed to engage student interest

Historical Imagination How it Can Work	Imagined History Cautions & Pitfalls
• Can engage students' interest and enthusiasm • Can make history and learning meaningful • Can highlight significant ideas, people, events, places or problems connected to the upcoming topic of study • Can highlight the useable past by ensuring that the most relevant details affecting actions, choices, context, &/or outcomes embedded in the hook are nearly identical to historical events to be studied, or that differences are carefully identified and consequences of those differences are explained	• Can eat up a lot of teacher preparation and classroom time without imparting significant historical content • Can promote a-historical "presentism" in an effort to make the upcoming topic of study "relevant" to students • Can lead to inaccurate conclusions about past eras or events if the hook misrepresents or strays too far from the real actions, choices, context and/or outcomes to be studied
▶ **Example:** **Present a set of paintings depicting the American Revolution. Use the prompt "What do you see?" to foster a free-flowing classroom discussion. Painting set could include images of different battle formations, soldiers with insignia of different nations, men & women, white & black in military service, as well as paintings made in different eras.**	▶ **Example:** **Divide the class into Patriots and British. Play a game of Capture the Flag in which the Patriot side is allowed extra time to hide the flag (to approximate the American's greater familiarity with the land).**
The visual imagery in a painting is generally accessible to students at all levels and provides information and ideas that students can use without prior knowledge. By carefully selecting images depicting different aspects of the war and different perspectives on the war this hook can serve as a good introduction to the multiple factions and perspectives they may encounter as the lesson progresses. Note: selection and discussion of artwork should include consideration of how the artist's perspective and own historical era may affect the accuracy and content of the image.	While it may be relevant to students' current play lives, Capture the Flag is not relevant to the American Revolution. Capture the Flag conveys fun and adventure. It cannot convey the physical dangers, high-stakes risks, multiple factions or multiple motives that characterized this seven-year struggle. It is a misleading and time consuming way to open the subject of Revolutionary War strategy.

Classroom Activity
Invited Guest

"Interview/ Listen to _____ about/talk about _____."

Historical Imagination How it Can Work	Imagined History Cautions & Pitfalls
• Can bring the past alive as real events, struggles and triumphs of real people • Can demonstrate the different ways people experienced the same event (due to personality differences as well as differences of age, gender, class, race/ethnicity, religion, region) • Can open a window on the long-term and unintended consequences of events • Can serve as starting point for examining differences between history and memory	• The experiences or perspective of an engaging classroom guest can be misunderstood as "the truth" or the most authoritative source about a historical event or era (invited guests speaking about their own experiences are a primary source) • Memories of past actions and feelings can be misunderstood as fully accurate recollections of past actions or feelings • Lack of information about the historical era or guest can result in class and guest time that is off-topic or fails to take advantage of guests' most valuable stories • Guest speaker's reflections about personal experiences which conveys "through their eyes" can be misused to draw conclusions about causes, effects and turning points.
▶ **Example:** **Panel of Vietnam era veterans and civilians speak to class about their experiences and attitudes during the War. Prior to class visit students and teachers provide guests with a set of pre-selected topics or questions. (Guests may be part of a single panel or speak to class at different times)**	▶ **Example:** **Vietnam War veteran speaks to the class about the War.**
Organized in this way students will have an opportunity to hear multiple perspectives, ensuring that the post-speaker conversation can address the multiple experiences and attitudes that made this such a difficult and contentious issue in the United States. Panels can be difficult to arrange; two carefully selected speakers can provide the needed breadth of perspective. (In the absence of at least two in-class guests one could modify this to include a viewing of taped interviews that provide other experiences and perspectives.) Pre-selecting topics or questions builds an important historical skill and prepares students and guest speakers to hone in on aspects of the event that matter most.	Lack of advance preparation by students and speaker can make it impossible for students to place the speaker's experiences in the context of the larger event. War stories from 1964, 1968 or 1971 can be inaccurate depictions for any other period of the war. Similarly, forces on the ground experienced a very different war from those serving in the air. Without advance preparation students might be insensitive to the possibility that the speaker has painful memories or be understandably hesitant to share an accurate story with children or strangers (silence might be expected on secret or illegal activities from the invasion of Laos to drug use to war crimes). If the speaker is presented as "the authority," his/her powerful stories can overwhelm other equally important or more accurate information.

Classroom Activity
Lecture
Teacher talks while students listen (may includes notetaking)

Historical Imagination How it Can Work	Imagined History Cautions & Pitfalls
• Can bring the past to "life" through engaging re-telling of past lives, challenges, struggles, triumphs and disasters • Can model historical literacy by explicitly incorporating and connecting elements of **TLH** to specific historical topics and issues • Can be organized to provoke reflection, analysis, questioning and use of evidence (opening with driving questions, using pauses for pair-share, 2-minute writes, student questions, examining sources) • Can demonstrate history as a conversation with the past and a conversation among historians	• Can lead students to believe that past and present differ only in detail (most likely when lecture consists of a fact-laden litany of people and events) • Can misrepresent history as a mass of facts to be memorized, rather than a discipline of inquiry and analysis • Often received by students as objective and the only account that matters (i.e. it will be tested as presented)
▶ **Example:** **Today's topic is the first industrial revolution, which began around 1780 in England and spread to parts of Europe and the United States by 1850. Our questions for the day will be:** • **Why did the industrial revolution begin in England? and** • **What was so "revolutionary" about the industrial revolution?**	▶ **Example:** **Today's topic is the first industrial revolution, which began around 1780 in England and spread to parts of Europe and the United States by 1850. I'll be explaining the new technologies and industries and the ways they changed how people lived.**
This introduction immediately engages students in **TLH** by framing the topic in terms of historical questions. These questions (which might be unit driving questions or lecture-specific questions) invite students to think about the lecture information as evidence and analysis rather than as facts to be memorized. This gives meaning to the lecture content AND challenges students to use the information as active learners rather than sit as passive listeners. This introduction models history as a conversation with the past. It presents the past as a time of uncertainty and change rather than a series of foregone conclusions. A teacher can use these questions as mid-lecture prompts for reflection, to check on student understanding and to promote use of historical sources.	This introduction prepares students to listen for and take notes on a list of inventions, industries, products and characteristics of peoples' lives. It leads students to expect a fairly simple and quiescent cause and effect relationship: new technologies and industries changed daily life. It does not require students to become engaged in the subject or suggest that industrialization was fraught with uncertainties, that it played out differently in different places and for different groups of people, or that understanding this historical era requires inquiry and analysis.

Classroom Activity
Letters or Diaries

"Assume you are _____. Write a letter to_____ ." or "Write a diary entry about_____."

Historical Imagination **How it Can Work**	Imagined History **Cautions & Pitfalls**
• Can prompt students to explore the personal, emotional, ethical and psychological dimensions of past lives and societies • Provides an opportunity to examine these types of historical sources, helping students understand that letters and diaries served different purposes in different cultures and at different time periods, as well as reflecting the thoughts primarily of literate classes of people. • Can serve as an assessment of students' understanding of the historical category of "through their eyes" • Teacher has collected sources or citations to direct research that students will need to inform their letters or diaries	• When students are instructed to enliven and personalize letters or diary entries they may draw ideas from their own values, worldviews and personalities (presentism) • Not well-suited for exploring certain kinds of complexity (e.g. letters do not generally identify or analyze long and short term causes of events; diaries reflect the private opinions of a single person even when the writer comments on the actions and motives of others) • Very difficult to capture the essence of daily life or personal concerns without substantial prior study of letters or diaries from the period under study
▶ **Example:** **You immigrated to the New York in 1900 when you were 20 years old. After 2 years you are sending money to your family in Italy so that your brother/sister can join you. What will you tell your brother/sister about how he/she should prepare for the trip and what he/she can expect to find in America?**	▶ **Example:** **You are a child in Italy in 1900. Write a letter to your best friend telling him/her that your family is moving to the United States. Tell your friend what you think about the move and what you are packing to take to America.**
Posed in this way the prompt directs students to consider what they have learned about emigrants' trips from Italy to the U.S. and about the experiences of Italian immigrants in the U.S. The information in the prompt guides students to use evidence about the living and working experiences of young Italian men or women. It encourages students to use historical imagination. Yet, by specifying concrete, verifiable experiences of the migration trip and life as an immigrant, the assignment can be evaluated for historical accuracy and historical understanding.	Students would need a great deal of prior knowledge about Italian society in order to imagine a historically accurate scenario (including poor Italian families' possessions, family roles, household traveling needs and likely modes of transportation and baggage). This writing prompt poses an unlikely historical situation: the vast majority of Italian emigrants to the U.S. in the late 19th and early 20th centuries were illiterate; most came from communities where friends communicated face-to-face. Without an ability or clear direction to accurately depict these aspects of Italian life c. 1900, students may draw on their own attitudes about moving away from friends and loss of personal possessions. Given these problems it's not clear how such an assignment could be evaluated for historical accuracy or an understanding of the immigrant experience.

Classroom Activity
Role Playing or Simulations

Students assume persona of _____ in the following situation_____.

Historical Imagination How it Can Work	Imagined History Cautions & Pitfalls
• Can serve as a capstone or integrating activity that allows students to use and learn from individual or small group research projects • Can provide an opportunity for students to connect particular experiences and perspectives to particular individuals or groups of people (based on class, gender, race, ethnicity, nationality, region, religion, education, political affiliation…..) • Can engage students in actively using historical sources to support arguments • Teacher has collected sources or citations to direct research that students will need to inform this activity • Can help students understand that the course of past events was not inevitable, but was shaped by the interaction of people, ideas, motives, material culture and differences in power to effect change • Debriefing after the activity should expose and/or correct historical inaccuracies, unresolved problems and ways in which the activity departed from the historical event or situation that was being simulated/role-played	• Focuses attention and places importance on what happens in the classroom rather than the real historical situation • Can eat up a lot of teacher preparation and classroom time without imparting significant historical content • Can reward students for passion, acting ability, leadership skill or creative imagination over depth of historical understanding and mastery of information • Requires significant advance preparation to ensure that students understand and can stay in character • Many significant historical events and situations cannot be accurately role-played or simulated because they involved physically or mentally dangerous conditions, they were affected by worldviews, beliefs or life-changing choices that cannot be reproduced in the artificial classroom setting

▶ **Example:**

Historical Issue: WWI, the U.S. and the sinking of the Lusitania in 1915

Simulation: Dinner Party conversation about "What will happen now?" following news of the disaster. Students are assigned roles as a 3rd generation German-American businessman, his 3rd generation Irish-American wife, & their rebellious daughter who joined the Socialist Party; a Democratic congressman & his sister who is active in the settlement house movement; an Anglo-American doctor, his wife who is active in the anti-suffrage movement, & their son who toured France in 1913 before starting college.

▶ **Example:**

Historical Issue: WWI, the U.S. and the sinking of the Lusitania in 1915

Simulation: Re-enact the German attack, sinking and news of the disaster in the U.S. Students are assigned roles as German commanders, German U-boat crew, captain of Lusitania, Lusitania crew, passengers, news reporters, U.S. President, and families of passengers.

Set up in this way the simulation focuses teaching and learning on historically significant aspects of the Lusitania sinking. It prompts students to articulate and discuss multiple reasons for and varying perspectives on the possible consequences of the Lusitania sinking. The selected roles expose historically realistic and researchable perspectives. In the process of exposing these different perspectives, this simulation can capture uncertainties and conflicts, challenging assumptions that the course of events was inevitable. Differences between the characters should contribute to a lively conversation that actively engages students and their historical imagination. Debriefing after the simulation can address students' use of sources to inform the conversation, perspectives not represented by the dinner party group (e.g. recent immigrants from nations already at war) and consider the difference between speculation about potential consequences in 1915 and what actually transpired over the course of the ensuing years.

This type of event may lead to a dramatic and engaging simulation. However, it poses a number of historical problems. Historically significant aspects of the Lusitania sinking cannot be simulated in the classroom (high-stakes tension, fear, uncertainty and real loss of life). Preparatory research for these roles could be very uneven. While the actions and thoughts of some of the assigned characters could be successfully researched (Lusitania captain, U.S. President, news reporters), others could be very difficult (U-boat commander and crew, Lusitania passengers and families). In the absence of sufficient historical sources students would be likely to draw on their own dramatic instincts, privileging acting ability and presentism over historical significance. Even in the absence of these problems, one needs to consider the educational value of a historically accurate simulation of this event. A simulation focused on the attack and sinking does not encourage consideration of the historically significant context (the Great War and U.S. neutrality) or of the consequences.

Classroom Activity
Film *(documentary or feature film)*
Students watch a film and take notes on a teacher-created viewing guide.

Historical Imagination How it Can Work	Imagined History Cautions & Pitfalls
• The power of visual imagery and a well-told story can grab students' attention, bring the past alive and make it meaningful • Can promote historical thinking by presenting perspectives, voices, and information that enhance or challenge other classroom and research sources • Showing excerpts or taking a limited number of planned pauses allows time for critically reflective discussion and analysis • Can provide opportunities to teach lifelong critical viewing skills, including consideration of filmmaker's point of view, reasons for making the film, intended audience, use of evidence and historical incidents, film techniques and "believability" based on the degree of agreement or departure from other historical accounts of the same events • Viewing guides can promote historical thinking by directing students' attention to use of evidence and interpretation • Reading scholarly film reviews can promote historical thinking by directing students' attention to use of evidence and interpretation	• Can occupy a lot of class time, particularly if show full-length film • Engaging and/or readily available film may be on topic, but cannot be used effectively by students because it is not directly relevant to historical theme(s), driving question(s) or key understandings • Feature films: Dramatic imagery and story line required for feature film success may depart so significantly from historical accuracy that students develop a misunderstanding of the past; film reviews written by historians provide crucial insight on these issues (see Resource Section) • The visual power and pace of the film medium can easily mask the fact that, like all history, it contains an interpretive perspective. The result can be an unquestioning acceptance of the film account as objective and true. (documentary and feature films) • Viewing guides can narrow students' attention to looking for answers; this is a particular concern if the guide asks for discrete facts or details. This type of viewing guide can discourage critical thinking and the ability to engage students in post-viewing discussions about larger themes, perspectives, use of historical sources, accuracy and interpretation

▶ **Example:**
Film Title: "The Long Walk Home"
Directed by Richard Pearce, New Visions Pictures, 1990. 97 minutes.

▶ **Example:**
Film Title: "Mississippi Burning"
Directed by Alan Parker, Orion Pictures, 1988. 120 minutes.

This film retells the story of the crucial Montgomery Bus Boycott of 1955–1956. The feature film format enhances this story; high production values and excellent performances by award-winning actors contribute to a compelling drama that captures the tensions, fears, dangers and uncertainties of the era. The story portrays fictional characters with historical accuracy. Complexities and nuances that would be difficult to tease out of primary sources and that would fall flat in a textbook rendition come alive in this film: struggles between personal beliefs and community values; conflicts within families (white and black); the evolution of race relations and of organizing strategies over the course of the year-long boycott; the interaction of gender and race on attitudes toward the boycott and integration; the personal risks and courage of bus boycott supporters; attitudes and strategies of the opposition. In addition, the film's accurate depiction of the bus boycott as a year-long grassroots movement involving thousands of people is an invaluable corrective to accounts that reduce the boycott to Rosa Parks' arrest or Martin Luther King's galvanizing speech at the Dexter Avenue Baptist Church.

This film is nominally about one of the many turning point events that punctuated the Black civil rights struggle in the 1960s - the disappearance and murder of three civil rights workers at the outset of Freedom Summer in 1964. Although students and teachers may find the drama compelling and the plot easy to follow, the film bears virtually no resemblance to reality. In this case the historical distortions are so central to the story and of such a magnitude that the film creates a lie rather than elucidating any truths. The film casts the F.B.I. as friend rather than active foe of greater civil rights; it depicts the struggle for civil rights as a contest between "good" whites and "bad" whites; it writes Black Americans out of the civil rights struggle in general and out of Freedom Summer in particular; it shows justice achieved through KKK-style terror. It would be very difficult to justify the class time needed to show this film AND to identify and correct its gross inaccuracies.

Checking Historical Literacy:
Historical Imagination or Imagined History?

Classroom activities that contribute to imagined history can be quite engaging. So can activities that promote historical imagination and build historical understanding. Sometimes it can be difficult to sort out the difference between the smoke and mirrors of the former (imagined history) and the real historical understanding that comes through the latter (historical imagination). The checklist below can help. **If your answers to the following questions are yes, then you're on your way to a historically literate lesson!**

_____ **History doesn't repeat itself.** Does the activity encourage students to consider that historical events occur in the context of the period studied, rather than representing a repeating cycle? Historians commonly look for patterns or similarities between events; at the same time they seek to understand the unique course of each event.

_____ **Avoids Presentism:** Does the activity ask students to evaluate or judge past actors or events in the historical context and circumstance, rather than being based on the morality, cultural norms, or popular beliefs of the present?

_____ **Avoids "What If?" history.** Does the activity encourage students to consider what did happen, rather than what could have happened if other events had taken place? (for example, What if the South had won the Civil War?) While often enjoyable and creative, the latter sort of exercise is a-historical because it asks students to imagine a time and circumstances that did not exist.

_____ **Change and Continuity.** Does the activity encourage students to see how the past is like the present, _and_ how it is also uniquely its own time and place?

_____ **Cause and Effect.** Does the activity consider unintended events and consequences in the past as well as those that were purposeful or intended?

_____ **Primary Sources.** Does the activity ask students to consider primary source material and make sense of those words, sounds or images in light of their historical contexts, and in relation to the larger theme or key understandings of the lesson?

_____ **Simulations.** If using simulations, am I careful to develop in students an understanding of how much we cannot experience and know of the actual historical actors who were participants in the event being simulated?

_____ **Film.** When using film, do I explore with students the historical accuracy of the film, and what the film says as an historical artifact itself? For example, what does _Little Big Man_ tell us about the historical events of the post-Civil War West, and what does it say about the US in the 1970's, when it was made?

_____ **Student voices.** Each generation of Americans interprets history in light of its own experiences. Does the activity take into account the questions my students are asking about the past?

_____ **Historical literacy.** Does the activity incorporate elements of historical literacy? Does it model and engage students in historical Questioning? Evaluation of evidence? Development of supported conclusions? Does it deepen students understanding of Cause and effect? Change and continuity? Turning points? Using the past? Through their eyes?

The Art of Asking Questions

Asking Questions to Promote Student Learning

What we ask students can have a more profound impact than what we tell them. Similarly, teaching students to question history can have a profound impact on how they learn. Rather than teaching students to accept everything they read or see as fact, we must teach them how to be inquisitive. Students should learn to raise questions about the history they are learning and they should learn to raise questions about the evidence used to reach those historical conclusions.

An important way to teach this is by asking questions that lead to investigation and analysis. Look for opportunities to provoke students into interpreting information and evaluating evidence. Create situations in which students must draw conclusions and support those conclusions from what they actually know.

- <u>Driving Questions to Guide Inquiry:</u> Pose a big question connected to the unit and ask students what they would need to know in order to answer that big question. Change the "what I'd need to know" statements into questions. Students can use these questions to guide their reading or research for the unit.

- <u>Primary Sources to Promote Investigation:</u> Give students a primary document that will be used later in the unit or lesson. Ask them what they do know and what they do not know from examining the document. The things they don't know can be formulated as questions for further investigation. Pictures, charts and tables work well for this because they are more readily accessible to students at multiple ability levels.

Course Plan:
Historical Themes
Big Picture

Unit Plan:
Driving Questions

Lesson Plan:
Key Understandings
Little Picture

 • **American Indians Before European Contact. Elementary School.**

TOPIC: American Indians Before European Contact

Historical Themes: (partial list)

• American Indians survived and thrived on this land's natural resources long before Europeans arrived

Driving Questions:

• What did the ancient Native people do for food and shelter?

• How was the Mississippian culture different from the woodland cultures?

• What happened to the Mississippian culture?

Key Understanding(s):
Students will be able to understand that –

• Native people occupied land in Wisconsin before Europeans came here.

• archeological evidence indicates that Mississippian culture farmed and built elaborate forts circa 1000BCE.

• historians and archeologists use found evidence, called artifacts, to create hypotheses about how people lived in the past.

I ask my fourth grade students to become historical detectives and investigate the mysteries surrounding the Mississippian people who once lived in a place we now call Aztalan State Park. I tell them that over a hundred years ago archeologists uncovered artifacts and remnants of structures including pyramid mounds that rose above a 22 acre site surrounded by a timber and mud wall in what is now Jefferson County. Scientists estimate that the ancient community may have been home to hundreds of people from 800BCE to 1200BCE. It's believed these people belonged to a larger culture since similar sites have been found in several states that have tributaries to the Mississippi River. In the late 1800s the site was identified as Aztalan because one hypothesis reasoned that these people were related to the Aztecs of Mexico. That hypothesis has since been dismissed since no evidence has been found to link the two cultures.

After learning that a hypothesis is an educated guess supported by evidence, students work in pairs and receive one question on a worksheet that requires each team to write their own hypothesis that is supported by factual evidence posted at our school "Mysteries of Aztalan" website.[15]

The questions include:

- What did the Mississippian people eat?
- What kind of housing did they build?
- Why did they choose this site for their homes?
- How were the objects pictured used by these people?
- Why did they have a fortress?
- What did they do with their dead?
- Why did they leave?

Student teams compare their hypotheses and debate the validity of their "facts" by asking questions such as "How do you know?" and "Why does that matter?" [See W-H-M Worksheet in Resource section] Since archeologists and historians have uncovered very limited information about these ancient people, there are few "right answers" to our questions. These budding historians learn to construct meaning from the artifacts of these ancient people. At the same time, this lesson is designed to help students understand that our state's oldest known civilization is shrouded in mystery leaving more questions than answers, much like history in general. We can imagine how things were for these people based on the limited archeological and historical record, but our findings will be mostly inconclusive.

My role as the teacher is to help students understand that ambiguities about the past are not uncommon. It is important to recognize historical uncertainty so that we don't make false assumptions such as linking the Mississippians to the Aztec culture without any real evidence. As we practice thinking like historians by using artifacts to construct an understanding of these ancient people, we learn to think critically about what we know and how we know it. Asking questions of the past helps my students develop an understanding of how historical knowledge is created. They also learn that their understanding of the past may change over time as more information is revealed.

[15] http://magee.kmsd.edu/%7Ekaldhus/aztalanhome.htm.

Course Plan:
Historical Themes
Big Picture

Unit Plan:
Driving Questions

Lesson Plan:
Key Understandings
Little Picture

 • *Second Industrial Revolution, U.S. High School.*

This lesson is part of a unit on industrialization in the late 1800s and early 1900s. The unit focuses on the multiple effects of industrialization, recognizing that different groups were affected in different ways. The lesson focuses on the rise of organized labor. Part of this lesson included an activity in which students read a set of primary documents related to work and unions during the second industrial revolution.[16]

Left to themselves my students might have been able to describe or summarize the content of each of the documents. I wanted them to do more than this. Students needed to use the content of the documents to develop the key understandings for the lesson.

I divided the class into three groups and assigned documents related to one union to each group (Knights of Labor, American Federation of Labor, and Industrial Workers of the World). In order to move my students to this higher level of document analysis I provided a list of primary source reading questions:

TOPIC: *Second Industrial Revolution, U.S.*

Historical Themes: (partial list)

- Economic change and development

Driving Questions:

- How did the second industrial revolution affect different groups?
- How did different groups respond to industrialization?

Key Understanding(s):
Students will be able to understand that –

- the rise of a mass, organized labor movement was a response to the changing nature of work.
- labor unions differed from one another (types of workers organized; attitudes toward immigrant, women and African-Americans workers; position on strikes; position on political reforms).

[16] This lesson was adapted from National Center for History in the Schools, *Bring History Alive! A Sourcebook for Teaching United States History*, (Los Angeles: NCHS, 1996), p. 137.

- How and why was this labor union established?

- What types of workers joined this union?

- How did the union view immigrants, African-Americans, Chinese and women workers?

- How did the union view factory owners and management?

- What position did the union take on the issue of strikes?

- What position did the union take on reform and political movements?

- Given the goals of the unions, what changes do you think were occurring in work and the economy?

- How did business management respond to union organization?

- How did business management respond to strikes?

- How did state and national governments respond to labor conflict?

After each group used their document set to answer these questions they completed additional activities that required them to use what they had learned to draw conclusions about organized labor during this era. Groups created a recruitment poster for their assigned union addressing the message of the union and the strategies the union promoted. They shared the posters with the class through a gallery walk. Then, each student used the same set of questions to draw a Venn diagram comparing and contrasting the three unions. This led to a class discussion focused on the key understandings.

Teaching Students to Ask Historical Questions

Asking questions about the past is not "natural." Students need to learn that they can and should ask their own questions about the past. Asking questions makes students more aware of why topics are relevant to a particular course, deepens understanding of each topic, and, ultimately, builds skills crucial to active citizenship. Students need practice at crafting meaningful historical questions. They can apply this skill across the curriculum to whatever they are studying.

When the objective is to develop question-asking skills it is not necessary for either the student or the teacher to answer all the questions. Making this clear from the beginning can create opportunities to discuss why some questions seem to matter more than others, why some questions would be more difficult to answer than others, and/or how one might go about researching an answer to different kinds of questions.

MODELING FOR STUDENTS

Teachers can help students understand that history always begins with questions by explicitly modeling how to question a textual passage, photograph or other historical source. Students learn good reading strategies when teachers demonstrate their own thinking out loud.

- Pause and insert questions while conducting a shared reading: "This makes me wonder..."

- Then, ask your students to do the same: "What does this make you wonder about?"

These questions teach students that reading is actually a conversation with a text. Practice as a group and discuss the quality of the questions. The **TLH** charts and rubric can be used to evaluate the quality of questions. The **TLH** charts gives students a basic set of historical questions to ask of any topic they may be studying, and is a good place to begin questioning history.

GENERATING STUDENT QUESTIONS

- <u>Using Sticky Notes:</u>
  Students can use sticky notes to literally have a conversation with the text. Encourage students to question their text and other reading sources. These might be broad questions, such as "I wonder why....?" Or, they might be focused questions, such as "What was a cooper?" Students can practice and become more proficient at generating questions by writing them on sticky notes and attaching the notes to the pages where the question occurs. Writing the questions slows down the readers as they monitor their own thoughts about what they're reading. Writing questions as one reads encourages rereading. Writing questions as one reads requires readers to evaluate information found in primary documents as well as textbooks. Eventually, students can remove the sticky notes and use their questions as a foundation for an assignment that analyzes the reading. Practicing reading strategies such as this will benefit students well beyond history class.

- <u>Using the</u> 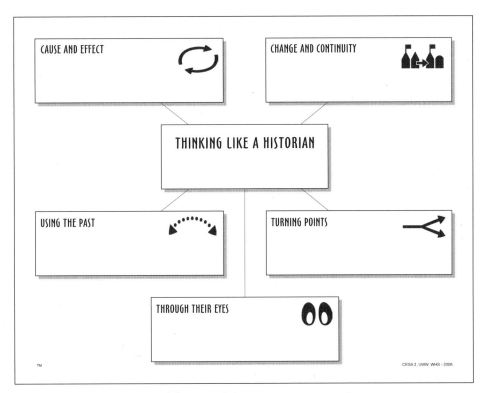 **TLH** <u>Worksheet:</u> Use the Thinking Like A Historian Chart Worksheet to help students formulate questions. Students should write the unit or lesson topic in the center box titled "Thinking Like a Historian." Then, ask students to write a question about the topic in each historical category of inquiry box. (Variation: divide the class into five groups and assign one historical category of inquiry to each group; student groups can be asked to write multiple questions for their assigned category) This exercise gives students practice using the **TLH** categories of inquiry. It prepares students to think about historical topics or events in terms of questions to be investigated, rather than as a mass of information to be memorized.

CAUSE AND EFFECT

CHANGE AND CONTINUITY

THINKING LIKE A HISTORIAN

USING THE PAST

TURNING POINTS

THROUGH THEIR EYES

CESA 2, UWW, WHS - 2006

[See full size worksheet in Resource section]

Course Plan:
Historical Themes
Big Picture

↓

Unit Plan:
Driving Questions

↓

Lesson Plan:
Key Understandings
Little Picture

- **American History: Founding Documents. Elementary School.**

Modeling for Students:

Teaching students how to ask good historical questions involves modeling how a historical detective might think. Good detectives look for what's not there as well as what is. I model this kind of questioning when my fourth grade students are studying the founding documents.

My fourth grade students read the first paragraph of the Declaration of Independence and selected parts of the United States Constitution. Of course, even carefully selected excerpts contain language that is unfamiliar to and difficult for many of my students. This becomes an opportunity to connect reading historical sources (reading in the content area) with the process of historical investigation. I model good historical questioning to help my students learn what the words and sentences mean. For example, I ask:

- "Exactly *who* was expected to be treated equally and given the right to life, liberty and the pursuit of happiness?" (The students often answer men.)

- "Men? Why not women?"

- "Did this Declaration include *all* men?"

When students discover that inalienable rights were limited to white adult male property owners, they are inevitably surprised that only a minority of people enjoyed full rights under the original government of the United States. Once students have arrived at this understanding I pose a new thread of historical questions about the "effects" of this situation.

- "How did different groups react to being left out or treated unequally?"

TOPIC: American History: Founding Documents

Historical Themes: (partial list)
- Founding Documents – Origins and Impacts

Driving Questions:
- Which peoples and groups were included in the Declaration of Independence?
- How did limiting full citizen rights to white men impact our country over time?

Key Understanding(s):
Students will be able to understand that –
- our country's founding documents originally limited full citizenship to white, property-owning men.
- many groups of Americans, including women, African Americans and Native peoples, have struggled to gain equal rights in this country for over 200 years.

Since this thread of questions cannot be answered by examining the Declaration of Independence or the Constitution my students are able to learn how answers to one set of historical questions can serve as the starting point for a new historical investigation. This investigative approach to the founding documents shows students that we can ask questions about even the most familiar things. Later, we can make cause and effect connections between the founding documents and major historical events such as the forced relocation of Native peoples, the American Civil War, the women's suffrage movement and the civil rights movement. Good questions lead to good connections.

 • *Questioning the Cold War. High School.*

Generating Student Questions:

After using the 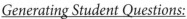 Chart Worksheet several times, my students were becoming familiar with how to write good historical questions, and how to get the knowledge needed to answer them. As we progressed through the semester, I tried a new technique. This time instead of asking students to complete a **TLH** Chart Worksheet I asked them to write questions on separate slips of paper. I turned one of my classroom bulletin boards into a large version of the **TLH** Chart Worksheet. Students stapled their questions on the bulletin board under the category they felt best represented their type of historical question. This served two purposes and had a very good unintended consequence:

- It helped my students identify which type of questions they had asked

- It led to a better discussion about the meaning of the **TLH** categories of inquiry

- Students realized that most of their questions fell into the categories of Cause and Effect and Through Their Eyes. As students discussed this they concluded that they had been taking the "easy" way out of questioning history. This led to much higher-order thinking from that point on.

TOPIC: Questioning the Cold War

Historical Themes: (partial list)

- Rise of the United States as a global power

Driving Questions:

- Why did the United States embrace internationalism after WWII?

- How did the United States use and project its power during the Cold War?

- How did American use of its global power affect people in other parts of the world?

Key Understanding(s):

Students should be able to understand that –

- the United States emerged from WWII as the world's most powerful economic and military nation and Americans believed that they had a responsibility and a right to prevent future world wars.

- during the Cold War the United States pursued policies at home and abroad that created, for the first time, a large military capability, greatly expanded trade and production in other nations and affected anti-colonial movements.

- nations of the world were divided into three general blocks (U.S. allies, Soviet allies, non-aligned); peoples in these nations did not always agree with their government's formal positions.

Analyzing Historical Sources

Teaching students to analyze historical sources bears some resemblance to generic best practice reading instruction. However, reading historical sources is not the same as reading a novel or a science text. Beyond the obvious fact that many historical sources cannot strictly be "read" (photos, maps, census data), it's important to keep in mind that primary and secondary historical sources have particular qualities that demand history-specific reading and analytical approaches.

Keys to Effective Teaching with Primary Sources

- **Understand the role that primary sources play in historical interpretation**. Primary sources are a building block of history, not history itself.

- Source or document **selection must be directed by a driving question**. All sources must be relevant to the driving question.

- **In order to understand the meaning and significance of a primary source it is necessary to evaluate key characteristics of all historical sources**, including: the role and perspective of the document creator, the intended purpose, the type of information or opinion conveyed and the extent of corroborating or conflicting evidence.

- **Primary source analysis must respect the historical concept of "through the eyes" of the creator and of the audience for the source.** Using present-day ideas, values, experiences, culture and lifestyles to understand the meaning of a historical source can lead to distorted or incorrect conclusions.

- **The end product of primary source analysis should be a historical interpretation, supported with evidence from the documents, that answers the driving question.** Analyzing a document(s) in isolation – without using that document(s) to develop or support historical interpretation – is only part of the historical process.

- **While some answers are clearly better than others, and some answers are clearly wrong, good historical questions do not have one right answer**. Good answers (good historical interpretations) are answers that are well-supported by the sources and do not exclude or ignore conflicting or difficult to understand sources.

- **Practice makes perfect** – well, not exactly "perfect" (see previous bullet point), but repeated analysis and interpretations of historical documents are the way to make history meaningful, engaging, and to build students' abilities to think like a historian.

Keys to Effective Teaching with Secondary Sources

- Understand the **role that secondary sources play in historical interpretation**. Secondary sources are examples of historical interpretation, whether the author(s) makes this obvious to the reader/viewer or not. Historians write journal articles and books (called monographs) that use their research in primary and secondary sources to support explicitly interpretive analysis of a specific historical topic or era. On the other hand, textbooks, encyclopedias and other summaries often provide quick overviews of historical events that can seem devoid of interpretation. They are not. Such overviews include interpretation through unseen decisions about what to include and what to exclude in order to satisfy space limitations (what matters) and by the choice of words used to describe a person or event (why does it matter).

- **Secondary sources are particularly valuable as resources for understanding historical context and major interpretive perspectives and historical controversies, as well as for locating additional sources on the topic.** These types of explanations and information are often overlooked by students and assignments focused too narrowly on factual details or "coverage."

- **Questioning the authoritative voice and interpretive conclusions in secondary sources is an effective way to develop critical reading and thinking.** Concise summaries often ignore historical controversy. Using secondary sources to practice asking questions of the text ("How do we know?") or comparing accounts of the same event in two or more secondary sources can be an effective lesson for teaching students to think like historians.

- **Secondary sources on the same topic can vary greatly. Select secondary sources and make decisions about which portions of a source to use based on how well those sources support larger course goals and driving questions.** It is not necessary for students to read an entire textbook simply because it's there. Short readings/viewings of non-textbook sources can provide essential information and ideas not found in a text or available primary sources.

- **While some secondary sources are more comprehensive or engaging than others, mastering the content of even the best secondary source is not the same as mastering historical literacy. Secondary sources, are essential building blocks of historical knowledge.** Information and ideas discovered in secondary sources help one develop and support historical knowledge.

Analyzing Evidence: Using Primary Sources Effectively

Students often have trouble understanding a time and its people. Primary sources can do a superb job of transporting students to the past, full of people and places profoundly different from their own time. Students can be challenged to think more deeply about both the past and the present as they grapple with the unfamiliar world revealed through primary sources. In order to do this, it is important to **read sources systematically**. This is an essential reading in the content area skill that can be embedded in lesson planning, instruction, and practice.

- Step 1: **"Source" the source.** Identify the creator, the date or time period, and, if possible, the purpose and intended audience.

- Step 2: **Establish context.** Use the sourcing information to describe the historical context within which the source was created. Use secondary sources and prior knowledge to do this. What important events or struggles were taking place at the time? Which groups of people or institutions were involved? What experiences, ideas and/or values from that time period could have affected either the content of the document or the ways different groups may have reacted to the document?

- Step 3: **Describe content.** "Describe" the information presented in the source. If it is a visual, what do you see? If it is textual, does it contain facts, opinion, analysis? Does it seek to record, inform, persuade, challenge? What specific information, ideas or opinions are conveyed?

- Step 4: **Make Connections.** "Analyze" the source by drawing connections between the source (step 1), the historical context (step 2), and the specific content of the source (step 3). At this stage the goal is to develop an understanding of the historical significance and meaning of the source. Remember that each source is like a single window on the past. What understanding of the past is glimpsed through this particular window?

- Step 5: **Evaluate the source.** Engage the source in a "conversation" with all the available sources – other primary sources, secondary sources, your prior knowledge. In what ways does it support, refute, challenge, or diverge from what you know about this topic from other sources? How much validity or weight is merited by this source when other sources are taken into consideration?

- Step 6: **Interpret the source.** "Interpret" all sources, using them as evidence to construct a supportable answer to your driving question.

Course Plan:
Historical Themes
Big Picture

↓

Unit Plan:
Driving Questions

↓

Lesson Plan:
Key Understandings
Little Picture

 Examples from the Field *Analyzing Historical Sources*

 • *Immigration and Westward Expansion, early 19th century. Middle School.*

I selected primary sources as I planned this 8th grade lesson [See Examples from the Field-Selecting Sources, above]. These primary sources included a copy of Stephen Austin's Second Colony Contract. As described earlier, I wanted students to use this primary document to help them answer the unit driving questions.

After introducing the lesson topic and driving questions and discussing the historical context for the primary document, I projected Austin's handwritten copy of the immigration contract on an overhead projector. I asked the class, "Who can read this document?"

A few students raised their hands. I asked select students to read the document aloud. Several of the students stated that they print and are unable to read cursive. A debate about cursive writing versus printing ensued. A few students explained that cursive writing was emphasized in elementary school, but they generally print. Other students, who print, stated they use computers, so they don't need to read or write cursive anymore. This became an unexpected lesson in change and continuity. It was necessary to use the typed version of Stephen Austin's Second Colony Contract so that all students could read it.

I formed ten groups and assigned one of the ten conditions from the contract to each group. First, I asked each group to explain their contract condition to the rest of the class. Each group's explanation was written on an overhead transparency for the rest of the class to synthesize. This allowed the entire class to consider the contract provisions as a whole. I asked: What contractual requirements did the Mexican government set for Anglos immigrating to Mexico in the 1820s?

TOPIC: *Immigration & Westward Expansion, early 19th century*

Historical Themes: (partial list)

• Immigration, motives and policies

Driving Questions:

• What policies did the Mexican government set for Euro-Americans immigrating to Mexico in the 1820s?

• How might those policies from the 1820s help us make sense of present day immigration?

Key Understanding(s):
Students will be able to –

• identify the requirements set by the Mexican government for Euro-American settlement in Mexican Texas.

• explain the kinds of citizens Mexico wanted the new immigrants to become.

• compare/contrast those immigration requirements to present day U.S. immigration requirements.

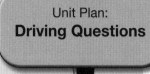

Course Plan:
Historical Themes
Big Picture

Unit Plan:
Driving Questions

Lesson Plan:
Key Understandings
Little Picture

What contractual requirements did the Mexican government set for Anglos immigrating to Mexico in the 1820?

- Must meet the requirements of the Colonization Law

- Families had 6 years to immigrate to the Second Colony land

- Families had to be industrious, have good morals and be Catholic

- Criminals, vagabonds and men of bad character could not immigrate. They would be deported.

- Colonists had to join a militia to keep out bad people. Austin would be the Chief.

- Mexican government would give land ownership and allow towns to be created after 100 families had immigrated.

- All communication had to be in Spanish. School had to be taught in Spanish.

- Churches had to be built. They had to have ornaments and vases for worship.

Next, I asked my students to develop a list of the ideals that were promoted by this set of contractual requirements. This would help my students think about connections between distinct requirements, such as the requirement that all communication had to be in Spanish, and the kind of society that might take shape if everyone followed the contract perfectly. It also provided a way to connect my students' own experiences with the seemingly distant past of the 1820s. Over half of my students are immigrants themselves, most emigrated from Mexico. The class came up with the following list:

```
Ideals promoted by Mexican government's
contractual requirements
• Maintaining a militia
• Acquiring the nation's language
• Gaining citizenship
• Educating the citizens
• Practicing religious beliefs
• Respecting laws
• Obtaining economic prosperity
• Having a strong family unit
• Exhibiting good moral character
• Owning one's own land and homes
```

The analysis of Stephen Austin's Second Colony Contract helped my students develop historical reading skills, and develop skills of primary document analysis. They also gained in-depth historical knowledge by analyzing a primary document in its historical context. Rather than viewing history in a vacuum my students were able to use this knowledge to draw conclusions about what has changed and what has remained the same.

- *Continuity*: They concluded that religious, economic, and cultural values desired by the Mexican government in the 1820s shared many similarities with the stated goals of the United States government today, and with the personal goals of Mexican immigrants to the United States today. They stated that immigrants might move to another country in order to obtain economic prosperity, but do not necessarily want to lose citizenship in their native country. When they thought about "continuity" they concluded that learning the host language, maintaining cultural values, securing employment, and purchasing a home remained constant over two centuries.

- *Change*: Students observed that some aspects of U.S. immigration policy today differ from those of the Mexican government in the 1820s. They generalized that immigrants today are not required to join the militia or practice a specific religion as a requirement to live in the United States.

Course Plan:
Historical Themes
Big Picture

Unit Plan:
Driving Questions

Lesson Plan:
Key Understandings
Little Picture

• **Indian History and Indian-Euro-American Relations. High School.**

Background:
I often give my high school students primary documents sets containing a variety of sources when we study topics that involve conflict between different groups of people or ideas. In this unit, titled *The Dispossessed, Immigration, and the City: America struggles with industrialization, 1865–1920,* students explore the ways that those outside the majority culture faced profound challenges following the Civil War. Students study African-American responses to Jim Crow segregation and the violence and degradation that attended notions of white, Anglo-Saxon race supremacy that became increasingly common in the late nineteenth century. Students explore American Indian responses to the dispossession of both their land and culture. During one part of the unit students view a film on Indian boarding schools and read secondary sources on reservation life and commonly held beliefs about race and evolution in that time period.

Using Primary Sources:
During one part of the lesson on American Indian responses I gave students a set of primary documents that included:[17]

- reflections of a member of the U.S. Department of the Interior's *Board of Indian Commissioners* regarding "race evolution"

- list of twenty-three rules for students attending Indian boarding schools

- images and photographs of American Indian children in and out of boarding schools

TOPIC: Indian History & Indian-Euro-American Relations

Historical Themes: (partial list)

- The role of women
- Religion in American history
- The role of ethnic and minority groups

Driving Questions:

- After passage of the Reconstruction Amendments, in what ways and why did powerful members of the dominant, majority American culture limit the rights of women, African-Americans, and American Indians?

- How did each of these groups respond in the face of loss of economic and educational opportunities, restrictions on cultural practices and beliefs, reduction of constitutional rights, and/or loss of tribal lands?

- What were the immediate and long-term effects of an attempted homogenization of American culture through assimilation of native peoples and immigrant groups?

Key Understanding(s):
Students will understand that –

- humanitarian groups and individuals sought to improve the lives of women and minority group members through a particular kind of education, assimilation, and the application of tenets that were middle class, Christian, and western (Euro-American) in their outlook.

- many Americans thought differently than we do today about race and culture in the late nineteenth century, and when acting on those beliefs, the effects were often oppressive, undemocratic, and damaging for minority group Americans.

I asked my students to read the rules and the comments of the Commissioner and examine the images. Then I led a class-wide discussion that examined the wording of the rules and the meaning of the notion of race evolution. For example, one rule reinforcing the importance of religious instruction stated that, "there shall be a Sabbath school or some other suitable service every Sunday, which pupils shall be required to attend." Another rule stated that Indian children "should be taught the sport and games enjoyed by white youth." Gender roles were important. According to the rules boys were expected to engage in vocational and agricultural pursuits, while "girls must be systematically trained in every branch of housekeeping."

I wanted my students to consider the past through the historical categories of *through their eyes* and *cause and effect*. I asked students a series of questions designed to reveal the thinking behind the rules. For example, "Why would white, well-educated humanitarians author and enforce these rules?" and, "What was the purpose of education in the late 19th century for those in the majority culture?" We also used the documents, particularly the images, to explore the effect of boarding school rules on American Indian children. I asked "What impact or effect do you think these rules, if enforced, might have had on children just recently removed from a very different culture?"

Students quickly moved from discovering what the documents "said" to analyzing and interpreting the larger subjects of Indian–Euro-American relations and the character of American society during the late 19th and early 20th centuries. Not surprisingly, a few of the students used "presentist" thinking and went no further than to conclude "this is horrible." However, most students began to raise their own questions and explore further. They asked questions about how people acted, the values and beliefs that motivated such actions, the nature of power and how power is exercised by different groups of people and how less powerful people or groups might struggle to maintain their identity, a concept that historians refer to as "agency."

[17] "Rules for Indian Schools, 1890," "Board of Indian Commissioner's Reports, 1905" in David M. Reimers, *The Way We Lived*, (Lexington, Mass: D.C. Heath, 1988) V.2; Photos available on-line at the Library of Congress and Wisconsin Historical Society.

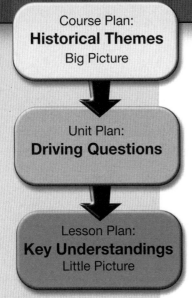

Course Plan:
Historical Themes
Big Picture

Unit Plan:
Driving Questions

Lesson Plan:
Key Understandings
Little Picture

Some of their questions included:

- Why were the boarding schools set up?
- Where did the prevailing, majority ideas come from?
- Were the boarding school rules consistently enforced?
- Were the boarding school rules successful?
- Did American Indian children and their families find ways around the boarding school rules to maintain their culture and integrity?

Although our discussion did not fully answer or address all of the questions, analyzing these documents stimulated my students' curiosity about the past, and about an episode in American history that few had known about. Students continued to expand their understanding that the past is complex and contradictory; that often the best of intentions may have disastrous consequences. They learned that separating the "good guys" from the "bad guys" is difficult and usually not particularly helpful if one is trying to understand past events and people. (The unanswered questions can be good starting points for special research projects.)

Such critical thought is difficult to achieve through passive instruction and secondary sources alone. Primary sources, when used well, bring the past alive in ways that excite historical thinking. Success requires careful teacher questioning, consistent student practice, and suspension of present-day judgments. Teachers must be prepared for exploratory and interpretive discussions that go in unpredictable directions and students must develop an openness of mind to travel to another place and time.

Developing Understanding

Developing an Understanding of the Elements of Historical Literacy

Developing understanding means developing historical literacy. This is best achieved and made "natural" by giving students the skills and tools needed to engage in the historical process and to investigate the past through historical categories of inquiry. As explained earlier, these are discipline-specific ways of knowing. Certainly students can and should take these critical thinking skills to other fields and endeavors. **However, teachers cannot presume that students will acquire historical literacy unless it is purposefully defined, modeled, taught, practiced and developed throughout their years in school.** The **TLH** framework can be a powerful tool in history education because it supports and fosters this kind of discipline-specific teaching and learning from kindergarten through university.

Developing understanding, like history itself, takes time. It also takes repeat experiences and practice. Do lessons, activities and assignments provide multiple opportunities throughout each unit and school year for students to:

- ask historical questions?

- gather evidence from a variety of sources?

- evaluate and analyze historical sources?

- interpret the historical record to arrive at their own, supported conclusion that explain or demonstrate what matters and why it matters?

- question and interpret the past through the patterns or lenses of historical categories of inquiry?

- ask questions and develop interpretations that investigate the depth and complexity of each historical category of inquiry?

WHAT - HOW - WHY WORKSHEET:

The W-H-W Worksheet can help students record and organize their evidence and thinking. The W-H-W Worksheet is a history-specific variant of the familiar KWL exercise. The Worksheet purposefully begins where most people begin when they answer a question, asking students to share what they "know." The second step, which asks "how they know," forces students to think carefully about the sources and accuracy of their knowledge. When students move to the second step they should record evidence that directly supports the answer in the first part. Success at this step is a sign of historical understanding. Lack of evidence, lack of sufficient evidence, or use of unrelated information is a sign that this type of historical understanding has not been achieved. Finally, the third step, which asks "why it matters," moves students to the level of historical interpretation. Students can demonstrate this element of historical literacy by connecting their knowledge to larger course themes, unit driving questions, related historical events, their personal lives, current events (using the past). An inability to explain why it matters is a sign that this type of historical understanding has not been achieved. The W-H-W prompts model good historical thinking and help to create teachable moments. The Worksheet can serve as a foundation for class or group discussion, student assignments, introductory hooks, or concluding exercises.

```
┌─────────────────────────────────────────────────────┐
│                                                       │
│         What – How – Why Worksheet                    │
│                                                       │
│   Historical Question:                                │
│   _____    │
│   _____ ?    │
│                                                       │
│                                                       │
│   What do we know?                                    │
│   _____    │
│   _____    │
│   _____    │
│   _____    │
│   _____    │
│                                                       │
│                                                       │
│   How do we know?                                     │
│   _____    │
│   _____    │
│   _____    │
│   _____    │
│                                                       │
│                                                       │
│   Why does it matter?                                 │
│   _____    │
│   _____    │
│   _____    │
│   _____    │
│   _____    │
│                                                       │
│                                                       │
│   Name _____ Date _____         │
│                                                       │
└─────────────────────────────────────────────────────┘
```

[Full size chart available in Resource section]

Developing an Understanding of the Past Through Historical Literacy

Historical understanding also means understanding past events, people, places and ideas in meaningful and useable ways. This is the point at which our students move from *acquiring* knowledge and skills to *applying* knowledge and skills. Teaching for this kind of historical understanding requires that student learning moves beyond a narrow focus on "what happened," to the more important determination of "what matters," and ultimately, to an ability to articulate "why it matters" (as well as when and for whom it matters).

Do lessons, activities and assignments provide multiple opportunities for students to draw on appropriate historical information and ideas to:

• explain or examine historical themes or driving questions?

• address real world interests, activities, problems or experiences ("using the past" to add perspective, depth, complexity, or suggest alternative approaches *and* avoiding presentism)?

• challenge, confirm or expand on historical conclusions put forward by others (classmates, movies, historians, books, family, news, political leaders….)?

Examples from the Field *Developing Understanding*

Course Plan:
Historical Themes
Big Picture

↓

Unit Plan:
Driving Questions

↓

Lesson Plan:
Key Understandings
Little Picture

 • *Is it War? Indian Removal in the early 19th century. Elementary School.*

My fourth grade students are exposed to more secondary sources than primary sources in their study of history because their reading ability is limited. Their textbook on Wisconsin's history describes events in easy to understand language, but the semantics chosen can impact the meaning of the passage. I want my students to analyze and question what they read about the past as opposed to simply committing what they read to memory.

One way I do this is to ask my students to compare and contrast two or more accounts of the same event. I begin by introducing the "name" of the historical event, and then I lead the class in a brainstorming session to produce a list of questions about the event. One such lesson is on an event often called the "Black Hawk War." When I introduce this subject I refer to it as the "Black Hawk Conflict." My students read two secondary accounts of the Black Hawk Conflict.

- 4th grade textbook description
- Wisconsin Historical Society, Turning Points website description

Our questions usually include the following:

- Who was fighting?
- What were they fighting about?
- What were they fighting against?
- Who won? How did they win?
- Where were they fighting?
- When were they fighting? How long did it last?
- Did it turn into a war?
- How did it change people's lives?

TOPIC: *Is it War? Indian Removal in the early 19th century*

Historical Themes: (partial list)

- Native people survived thousands of years on natural resources
- Early European explorers, traders & immigrants changed Native people's lives
- Government forced Native people to relocate

Driving Questions:

- What happened to Black Hawk's people at the Bad Axe River?
- Was it war or something else?
- Why are these accounts different?

Key Understanding(s):
Students will be able to understand that –

- Native people were forced off land that was then settled by European immigrants and Yankees moving west.
- historical accounts can be different.

Course Plan:
Historical Themes
Big Picture

Unit Plan:
Driving Questions

Lesson Plan:
Key Understandings
Little Picture

After each reading students attempt to answer the class questions based on the information provided in that account of the conflict. I want my students to be active, questioning readers. So, I encourage them to use hi-liters to illuminate their answers, and to write new questions that might arise while reading. They could write questions on sticky notes or in the margins. (Students were reading from copies, not the textbook itself.)

Next, I asked student to compare the two versions of the event and decide which one provided better answers to their questions. This generated a wonderful class discussion. Students discussed the difference between a war and a massacre since both words were used to describe the event. They tried to decipher from the two accounts which word, war or massacre, better describes the 1832 battle at Bad Axe River.

To assess their understanding, I asked students to write short-answer essays that ask about different steps in the historical process. I asked:

- How does word choice impact the telling of a story? (evaluating and analyzing evidence)

- Which account gave you a better understanding of the Black Hawk conflict? Why? (evaluating and analyzing evidence; determining what matters and why it matters)

- What can we do to learn more about what actually happened in the past? (asking questions; evaluating and analyzing evidence)

TOPIC: *Camp Life During the Civil War*

Historical Themes: (partial list)
- Experiences of soldiers during times of war

Driving Questions:
- Why would anyone lie so that they could join the Civil War?

Key Understanding(s):
Students will be able to –
- identify differences between past and present.
- ask historical questions based on reading about the topic.
- use evidence from primary and secondary sources to answer their own historical question.

• *Camp Life During the Civil War. Middle School.*

"Lying To Serve Your Country" – Using **TLH** to create a Teachable Moment

The Setting:
I wanted to engage my students in this unit by using examples from real soldiers. So I collaborated with the language arts teacher at my school to find readings on the life of soldiers during the American Civil War. We discovered an eclectic compilation of historical readings in the literature book. One selection, excerpted from Bruce

Catton's book *Reflections of the Civil War*, contained a wealth of information about the camp life of soldiers.[18] There was an accompanying audio recording. My students were surprised that a history teacher was using literature books to teach a history class.

I instructed my middle school students to read silently as the narrator described the historical players who fought and died in one of the most horrific wars in United States history. As they read and listened my students heard that most people believed that the war would be short and that the war was first greeted with parades, picnics, and marching bands. As the war dragged on both the North and South were drained of resources, energy, and lives. Most of the soldiers who enlisted or were recruited came from small towns and were farmers. Over 600,000 men died in this war. Most deaths were due to dysentery, measles, typhoid fever and other camp diseases. About one-third of the deaths were combat related. As the war began, neither the Northern soldiers nor the Southern soldiers had adequate uniforms, weapons, or supplies. Nevertheless, enthusiastic teenagers from the backwoods, cities, and countryside lied about their ages in order to join the army.

The Teachable Moment:
My students became engaged in the real life stories. Although the age requirement for a Civil War soldier was eighteen, young boys were eager to enlist. Catton explained that many boys, not wanting to lie under oath to a government official, used a subterfuge:

> It turned out that, in the North at least, a very common little gag had developed.
> A boy who was under eighteen and wanted to enlist would take a piece of paper
> and scribble the figures eighteen on it. Then he would take off his shoe, placing
> the piece of paper into the sole of his shoe, put it back on and tie it up. He would
> go to the recruiting station, and since he would obviously be looking rather young,
> sooner or later the recruiting officers would look at him and say, "How old are you,
> son?" Then the boy, in perfect honesty, could say, "I am over eighteen."[19]

At the end of the reading-recording, one of the male students said, "I don't get it. Why would anyone lie so they could join the Civil War?" A chorus of voices joined in to support this assertion. Several students said there is no way they would lie in order to serve in the war in Iraq or any other war for that matter.

This was a good example of students seeing the world "through 21st century eyes." The war they read about in the newspapers and the war images they see on television are frightening and involve death. They were dumbfounded that under-age males would lie in order to serve their country during a declared war.

---

[18] Bruce Catton, "Reflections on the Civil War," in Arthur Applebee, *The Language of Literature* (McDougall Littell: Evanston, Illinois, 1997), 46–53.
[19] Ibid., p. 48.

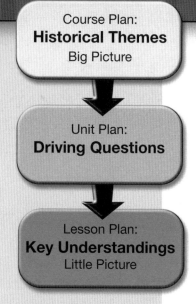

Course Plan:
Historical Themes
Big Picture

Unit Plan:
Driving Questions

Lesson Plan:
Key Understandings
Little Picture

Using **TLH** *to Recognize and Capitalize on a Teachable Moment:*
Luckily, there was a **TLH** Chart on a bulletin board in the classroom. As students struggled to comprehend why anyone would have lied in order to fight in the Civil War I pointed to the *through their eyes* category and asked:

> "What evidence is provided in the selection that would help us understand the reasons why the boys lied to fight in the Civil War?"

Next, I pointed to the *using the past* category and asked:

> "How was the Civil War different from wars being fought today?"

A quick review of the selection revealed important differences between past and present:

- The war was celebrated during the 1860s with parades, music, and flag waving.
- This was a way to advertise to the citizens that war was patriotic, adventurous, and noble.
- The passage reveals that the war would be over in less than a month so the boys believed that they would fight for only a short time period.
- The Civil War was fought on American soil and the boys wanted to defend their families.
- Peer pressure may have influenced their decision. Many friends and relatives enlisted together.

By using the **TLH** Chart and categories of inquiry, I learned that my students were beginning to think like historians. They formed their own essential question and then searched for information to answer it. The class engaged in historical dialogue that day. My students were able to use the evidence from this reading selection to answer their own question:

- Lying allowed an under age recruit to defend his country and achieve a "greater good."

- Conversely, present day wars are not met by the kind of fanfare that might build enthusiasm as in the Civil War; my students' real life experience is of a long war; recent American wars have been fought far away from American borders; there is no peer pressure to lie; it's not likely that a person could get away with this kind of lie today.

• *Investigating History and Commemoration. High School.*

After a trip to Washington D.C., I wanted to be able to discuss with my high school students the different memorials and monuments that I had visited. I didn't want them to just see the photos and discuss what they looked like, but to dig deeper. Who built them? Why were they there? Where did the money come from? What questions do they raise? What was happening during the time the memorial was built? What historical interpretation was conveyed by the way the event was memorialized? Are any monuments "missing," and if so, why?

I created a poster board for each memorial I had visited in Washington D.C, using my photographs as well as historical information and brochures from the monuments themselves. I displayed these around my room and asked students to go on a "gallery walk" at their own pace. I instructed students to look at the information and then complete a worksheet based on the questions above. They used these questions to guide their analysis of each poster. I also asked students to write questions connected to two **TLH** historical categories of inquiry for each of the memorials.

TOPIC: *Investigating History and Commemoration*

Historical Themes: (partial list)

- Wars have unintended and unanticipated consequences.
- Wars have been significant turning points

Driving Questions:

- Why are historical monuments built?
- Do monuments tell accurate histories of the event memorialized?

Key Understanding(s):
Students will understand that –

- historical monuments in Washington D.C. have been built long after the event that is memorialized.
- historical monuments often convey as much about the time period in which they were built as about the event memorialized (e.g. Lincoln Memorial, built during era of Jim Crow, ignores slavery; WWII Memorial, conveys 1990s fascination with the "good war," the "greatest generation," and the U.S. as a global power).

My students had wonderful conversations about the size of some memorials in relation to others, what was chosen to be memorialized and by whom. They were able to use the historical knowledge they gained in earlier lessons as background information to draw their own conclusions and continue to question history. While discussing the Lincoln Memorial, one student asked why Lincoln appeared to be sitting on a throne - an amazing observation for a fifteen year old. This led to a discussion about the time period in which it had been built and the social climate during the 1910s and 1920s - things my students never would have thought to question or discuss from looking at a picture in a textbook.

This culminating activity required students to consider what they had learned about each of the wars memorialized by a monument in the nation's capitol. It required students to examine the monuments as artifacts representing the era in which each was built. Finally, by asking about the historical interpretation conveyed by each monument students were led to a deeper understanding of both the wars themselves and the ways in which Americans remember that past.

Assessing For Understanding

Assessment needs to be ongoing. Assessment of historical understanding, like assessment of other kinds of knowledge, should occur on two levels. *Formative assessment* comes from multiple sources, including small-group discussion, whole class discussion, exit cards, pretests, teacher observation, questioning, self-reporting, and assignments.[20] At the end of a unit, teachers can use a variety of *summative assessments* including selected responses, constructed responses, and performance based responses such as presentations, debates, and simulations.

Teachers can use the **TLH** framework to translate generic best practice assessments into effective history-specific assessments of understanding.

Assessment Components	Effective History Assessments
Meets learning objectives	Ask students to respond to one or more of the unit driving questions – OR to respond to a student-friendly version or subset of the unit driving question(s)

Requires demonstration of content knowledge	• Require the use of specific and accurate information, ideas and sources
	• Require demonstration of proficiency in one or more historical category of inquiry
	    • Cause and effect
	    • Change and continuity
	    • Turning points
	    • Using the past
	    • Through their eyes
	• *Summative assessments* should elicit level 3–4 responses on the **TLH** Rubric for Historical Categories of Inquiry

Requires demonstration of skills	• Require demonstration of proficiency at one or more historical process skills
	    • Asking historical questions
	    • Gathering sources and evaluating the evidence in those sources
	    • Drawing conclusions, supported by evidence, to answer a historical question
	• Summative assessments should elicit level 3–4 responses on the **TLH** Rubric for Historical Process Skills

Provides an opportunity to reflect upon learning	Allow students to
	    • Connect what they have learned to prior knowledge and/or to their own lives
	    • Avoid "presentism"

Rubric assesses quality of student understanding, not quantity of student output	Use grading rubrics that assess understanding and skills that would score 3–4 on the **TLH** Rubrics • Note: the **TLH** Rubrics are intended as Instruction and Assessment Planning guides for teachers; teachers may want to use elements from these to construct grading rubrics that are developmental and topic appropriate.

[20] Exit cards: Students must turn in a card with a new fact or question before leaving the class. This strategy can also be used as an entrance ticket.

Examples from the Field *Assessing for Understanding*

Course Plan:
Historical Themes
Big Picture

Unit Plan:
Driving Questions

Lesson Plan:
Key Understandings
Little Picture

• **Government Policy and Indian Removal. Middle School.**

After completing an eighth grade history unit about President Andrew Jackson's policy toward American Indians, I wanted the students to complete a summative assessment that would demonstrate their ability to answer the driving questions. My students had worked on editorial writing in their language arts class, so I decided to construct an assessment that took advantage of that writing experience.

I wrote a short prompt for the editorial:

> *Assume the persona of an American newspaper editor in the 1830s. Write a one-page editorial that expresses your opinion about the Indian Removal Act of 1830.*

By itself this prompt would not have produced very good editorials or allowed me to assess a student's understanding of this historical era. So, in addition to this short prompt the assessment included important guiding requirements.

TOPIC: Government Policy and Indian Removal

Historical Themes: (partial list)

• Migration leads to cultural diffusion
• The expansion of the U.S. affected different groups in different ways

Driving Questions:

• Why were American Indians forced to move away from their lands?
• What were the consequences of forced removal?

Key Understanding(s):
Students will understand that –

• political, economic and social factors motivated the U.S. policy of Indian Removal.
• Native people resisted removal because it would destroy their communities, mean the loss of their land and resources, and violated the stated ideals of the United States.

Course Plan:
Historical Themes
Big Picture

↓

Unit Plan:
Driving Questions

↓

Lesson Plan:
Key Understandings
Little Picture

- Develop a persona for yourself and your newspaper that locates your paper in a real place and that includes likely personal characteristics of a newspaper editor in 1830s America. Attach this to the editorial.

- Review all the information you have from this unit before writing the editorial (textbooks, maps, notes, diaries and government documents).

- As you prepare to write the editorial think about political, economic and social reasons your newspaper editor might support or oppose the Indian Removal Act. [note: Although an editorial writer would not specifically use these terms, I had been using them throughout the semester; they are important for students to learn and use in all history lessons]

- Use historical imagination to explain your position through the eyes of your newspaper editor of the 1830s.

- Use specific ideas, terms, attitudes, and factual details from the early 1800s to explain and support your editorial opinion.

This was a complex lesson for my eighth grade students. During the unit they had examined a number of different sources and different perspectives and experiences. Some of their sources presented the voices of government officials and others involved in making policy and forcibly removing Native people. Other sources presented the voices of American Indian leaders and the people who resisted U.S. government policy. They needed to master a lot of detail, develop an understanding of how different groups of people in the 1830s felt about this policy, and try to use terms that are not commonly used today. I adapted this assessment for students with emergent writing skills. My students mastered some of these skills and understandings better than others. The assessment helped me pinpoint both their strengths and their weaknesses. For example, my students need more practice inquiring about, investigating, and using the historical category of *through their eyes*. I was able to pinpoint some of the assessments' strengths and weaknesses as well. For example, the editorial format led students to speak through the voice of Euro-Americans even when they were using information and arguments expressed by Native people in their sources.

Excerpted Student Responses	Teacher Reflection on Student Learning
"They were here first, simply put. They work just as hard as the average American if not much more. Indians have been in touch with the nature of the this land for more than a millennium and one day we come in and try to take it away from them. That's not right." "…The Indian Removal Act of 1830 is trying to force a new culture upon them, while forcing the Indians into a confined remote part of the country…" "We should work with the Indians in a manner that respects what they believe…" "Why not include the Indians in our society because they were here first?" Daniel	Consequences of Removal: understands that cultural diffusion would occur when Native people were forced from their homelands. - - Native peoples' lives will be forever changed as they are confined to a remote part of the country; Indians have been in touch with the nature of this land…. Social motives: understands that U.S. policy makers are motivated by social and cultural beliefs that the Native people were inferior and would be "better off" if they were more like Euro-Americans. - - "trying to force a new culture upon them" Economic motives: some sense that Euro-Americans want the economic resources of Indian land - - removing them to remote part of the country; living together and sharing the land would be better Problem: Presentism. reasons for opposing removal are 21st century ideas about fairness, multi-cultural cooperation. Does not use language or terms reflecting through their eyes understanding Problem: No real historical details or evidence here. Refers to Native people as a single group (they..).
"…We also are removing them because of religious differences. Andrew Jackson is saying that they have no form of government, no religion, and no writing systems, which has been proven false. Andrew Jackson is saying they have none because they differ from our beliefs and customs. He says since they are not Christian or have a different way of running their civilization, that they are savages. No good reasoning could have resulted in such false accusations. This act is simply unfair and humiliating for the sensible settlers. It questions our intelligence by telling us to think that this act will better both civilizations. Well it won't. It will only help us. It will give us land and take land away from them. I think this vile act is inadequate and won't solve our problems. It is the coward's way out." Alexandra	Consequences of Removal: general sense that this will be bad for Native people, but not much detail; hints at conflict - - won't solve our problems. Cultural diffusion: recognizes that Native people have strong cultures, beliefs and customs that differ from Euro-Americans - -no good reasoning, not being Christian means they are savages. Concluding statement implies that once the law is enacted the lives of both nations will be forever changed. Social motives: good understanding of religious differences and educational levels as a stated, but false difference (Christianity, writing systems) Economic motives: infers that land has value and U.S. wants it for economic reasons - - will give land to us, take land away from them, will only help us. Use of sources: makes some effort to identify specific arguments and people - - Jackson, claims that Native people had no religion, writing system, govt. Through their eyes: makes a good effort to use words that suggest 1830s instead of 2006 – "that they are savages" "no good reasoning…" "sensible settlers" "vile act" Uses idea of "truthfulness" to oppose the policy - -questions our intelligence Problem: Presentism: uses 21st century ideas of fairness and multi-cultural respect to oppose the policy

Course Plan:
Historical Themes
Big Picture

↓

Unit Plan:
Driving Questions

↓

Lesson Plan:
Key Understandings
Little Picture

Formative Assessment:

My high school U.S. history class was studying WWII. I needed a quick assessment to determine whether my students understood the ideas, beliefs and practices that were central to that conflict. A traditional quiz might ask students to match words to definitions or write short definitions that would essentially test their ability to recall someone else's explanation. Instead, I wanted to know what those terms meant to my students and if they understood the meaning of those terms in the context of the 1930s and 1940s.

I decided to ask my students to create a visual representation of some key terms. Students partnered up. I gave each pair a term and asked them to write a definition of their assigned term and explain its relation to WWII. Then, I instructed each group to draw a visual representation that they felt explained the term. They drew the visual on one side of a sheet of paper and wrote their definition on the other side. Students then presented their pictures to each other. Classmates had to guess which terms were being demonstrated through the pictures. Student pairs could not use words to explain their drawing.

While my students became enthusiastic about this kind of creative activity, I was happy to see that they put a lot of thought into how they were going to represent their term. My students could not simply copy or paraphrase their textbook or my lectures to complete this assessment. They had to use the historical information they had learned, think deeply about how these ideas and concepts had affected events during the 1930s and 1940s, and then express this understanding in their own "picture words."

TOPIC: _Politics and Diplomacy During World War II_

Historical Themes: (partial list)

- Ideas and beliefs affect how people and nations act.

Driving Questions:

- How did certain ideas and beliefs connect one historical event to another?
- How did these ideas and beliefs contribute to turning points in history?

Key Understanding(s):
students will be able to –

- define influential political ideas and practices related to World War II (alliance, appeasement, imperialism, fascism, communism).

- connect these terms to historical events, actions and people (relate appeasement to the pre-war British and French effort to contain German expansion, relate fascism to the Nazi Party, German expansion and the Holocaust...).

- demonstrate how these ideas and practices contributed to turning points in history (appeasement allowed Hitler and Germany to invade neighboring countries, setting off war in Europe; fascism provided justification for territorial expansion, for destruction of German democracy and for the Holocaust).

Parting Thoughts

Thinking Like a Historian offers the **individual teacher** a conceptual understanding of history as a discipline and a pedagogical framework to support the highest quality and most engaging history teaching and learning. We hope that you find this framework helpful in placing history teaching at the center of social studies education. For many of our readers *Thinking Like a Historian* has reenergized the passion they have for this anchor discipline.

***Thinking Like a Historian* can also be a practical resource for professional growth and development**. We encourage you to use it for this purpose. It can be used:

- as the centerpiece of individual reading and reflection

- by mentor teachers working with entry level educators

- in unit, team or department meetings as a component of program review or development

- as the focal point for a History Retreat where school or district teachers rethink how and what they teach

We offer one piece of advice. Encourage your colleagues to read this guide in its entirety. As you ponder the first reading you will realize that its arguments, premises and examples are interrelated. It's essential to gain a sense of this whole before "pulling out" a favorite lesson or teaching idea. Examples from the field are meant as concrete demonstrations of the ideas and practices incorporated into the **TLH** framework. They are not designed or presented as off-the-shelf, ready-to-use lesson plans.

The authors of *Thinking Like a Historian* have incorporated **helpful checklists, charts and rubrics** that can be used to assess specific components of historical literacy, history teaching and history learning. Some of these are designed specifically for planning and reflection. The final worksheet is a **TLH** Inventory that can be used to assess the strengths and weaknesses of history teaching in your classroom or school. Other charts and worksheets are designed for classroom use. All charts, worksheets and rubrics that appear in small size in the body of this guide are included in full size in the Resource section that follows. The Resource section also includes a brief guide to history teaching resources and professional growth opportunities, as well as a glossary of history-specific terms.

Finding Teaching Materials and Resources — *You Can Surf and Never Find a Beach*

Lesson Planning

- American Historical Association

  http://www.historians.org/

  This professional organization welcomes historians from all fields and is increasingly opening its doors to K–12 teachers. The AHA publishes a series of pamphlets and short books, written by leading historians, for history educators from upper elementary through university levels. These publications provide succinct analyses, teaching ideas and resource bibliographies for significant historical topics and teaching methods, ranging from teaching the history of women in early modern Europe to teaching history with film.

- National Center for History in the Schools

  http://nchs.ucla.edu/

  Headquartered at UCLA and headed by historian Gary Nash, the National Center for History in the Schools provides resources for teaching standards-based lessons in both US and World history. This site shares online, at no-cost, the *National History Standards*, which support a history scope and sequence. Ordering information is provided for *Bring History Alive*, available in both *US and World History* editions and for *Lessons from History: Essential Understandings*. These publications offer background and thematic essays on significant historical topics, historical themes, driving questions and essential understanding directly applicable to K–12 history curriculum. In addition, these and other NCHS publications include high quality standards-based lessons, authored by teachers.

- Library of Congress

  http://memory.loc.gov/learn/

  The Learning Page within the Library of Congress, American Memory Collection site offers a wealth of resources, ranging from dozens of lesson plan ideas linked to accessible primary resources to document analysis worksheets you can use in the classroom.

- Organization of American Historians, *Magazine of History*

  http://www.oah.org/pubs/magazine/

  This professional organization is committed to teaching history and building a firm relationship between the university and K–12 communities. The OAH provides a number of resources and benefits for history educators, including reduced membership and conference fees, and online resources to support history in the schools. Membership includes the superb bi-monthly *Magazine of History*. Each issue focuses on a different historical topic, providing up-to-date summaries of the historical topic, the latest scholarship, primary documents, lesson plans and worksheets, teaching ideas, bibliographies and more.

- National Archives and Records Administration

  http://www.archives.gov/publications/prologue/

  By providing ready access to many of America's most important and intriguing documents, the National Archives supports educators with web-based lesson plans, document analysis sheets for a variety of source types, and information about professional development opportunities. The site's lesson plan section contains reproducible copies of primary documents organized in chronological units. Additionally, these lessons are correlated to the National History Standards and National Standards for Civics and Government, as well as identifying interesting cross-curricular connections.

- Center for History and New Media

  http://chnm.gmu.edu/category/teaching-and-learning/

  The Center for History and New Media is sponsored by George Mason University and is supported by several national grants. This site offers best practices in history teaching and learning. The CHNM's *National History Education Clearinghouse* links to website reviews, teaching materials and more.

Primary And Secondary Sources

- Film Reviews and Film Criticism Resources

  http://www.lib.berkeley.edu/MRC/filmstudies/reviewslist.html

  Maintained by the Film Studies Department at the University of California, Berkeley, this site provides strategies for finding films and film reviews, links to film reviews and access to a select number of film indexes.

- Gilder Lehrman Collection

  http://www.gilderlehrman.org/

  Another remarkable resource, the Lehrman Collection includes *History Now*, an online guide that focuses on a different historical subject each month, and provides document-based lesson plans for elementary, middle and high school. The page for teachers and students contains a number of resources, including selected documents and activities, and historians' pod casts discussing their work.

- History Matters

  http://historymatters.gmu.edu/

  A joint endeavor of CUNY's Graduate Center and George Mason University, this impressive site provides access to 1,000 primary sources, a section dedicated to how historians evaluate and analyze sources, and an annotated list of 1,000 history websites. Among other related resources, teachers will find the *Digital Blackboard*, an exhaustive collection of web-based teaching assignments, most rooted in numerous primary sources. Also see a companion project, Historical Thinking Matters, http://historicalthinkingmatters.org/ The Historical Thinking Matters website is a collaborative project with Stanford University and others that provides engaging and challenging activities designed to boost students' historical thinking skills and their ability to analyze and use primary sources.

- Library of Congress

  http://memory.loc.gov/ammem/index.html

  When seeking a primary source that fills a particular need within a unit or lesson, teachers will find that the American Memory Collection can help them find the right document quickly, particularly if the subject is related to U.S. history. A powerful search engine quickly explores the 7 million primary sources in our nation's largest collection of digital documents. These include a vast range of photographs, moving pictures and maps, as well as print material ranging from letters to broadsides to newspapers. The LOC is also adding seamless links to documents at highly respected archives around the country. Like other sites, this one contains a valuable section with teacher-designed and classroom-tested lessons that center on the use of primary sources.

- National Archives and Records Administration

  http://www.archives.gov/historical-docs/

  In addition to providing ready access to and teaching support materials for many of our nation's most important documents (see annotation above), the National Archives also produces many publications, including *Prologue Magazine* (http://www.archives.gov/publications/prologue/), a quarterly magazine that brings to life many of the documents held by the archives. Back issues containing fascinating explorations of documents are available online, or through subscription.

- National History Day

  http://www.nationalhistoryday.org/

  National History Day is a nationwide event that engages teachers and students in exciting historical research and interpretation. The national organization selects a new theme for each year that guides students' development of research topics and questions. National, state and regional NHD sponsoring agencies and coordinators offer a wealth of information about how and where to find historical sources. Participants in the NHD competitions select a topic of interest within the annual theme, learn how to frame good historical questions, find, evaluate and use primary and secondary sources, and to draw and present supportable historical conclusions.

- Public Library in your local community

  Local public libraries are often rich repositories of primary source material, including local and state newspapers, local government records, and numerous community resources, such as business directories and maps. Many public libraries are connected with local or county historical societies, and have access to broad holdings through interlibrary loan.

- Wisconsin Historical Society

  http://www.wisconsinhistory.org/

  Considered by many the finest repository of North American materials in the world, the Wisconsin Historical Society is dedicated to providing online access to thousands of documents in a number of collections. Two on-line collections are of particular value to teachers: *Turning Points*, which offers brief historical essays supported by hundreds of primary sources organized by the major historical eras spanning American and U.S. history, and *American Journeys*, which provides on-line access to thousands of documents related to early exploration and settlement throughout North America. Teachers will discover excellent teaching resources on this site, including lesson planning guides focused on Wisconsin history. The majority of its vast collections are housed at the WHS Archives in Madison. The WHS offers unprecedented public access to much of that collection through Area Research Centers across the state (many at UW campuses). Wisconsin teachers can find primary sources of local interest, or request holdings from other sites through inter-library loan.

Professional Development Opportunities

- History Matters

  http://historymatters.gmu.edu/

  To better understand document interpretation, *History Matters* provides teachers with "Making Sense of Evidence," a section of the site that encourages teachers to explore eight different kinds of primary sources ranging from maps and films to advertisements and photographs. An associated page called "Scholars in Action" asks teachers to interpret a useful and interesting document, and then listen to an audio clip in which noted historians explain how they read the source. This is an excellent self-directed professional development experience in primary source interpretation skills that will pay dividends in the classroom.

- Library of Congress workshops

  http://memory.loc.gov/learn/educators/index.html

  Teachers interested in enhancing their classroom use of primary sources and historical investigation will discover much value in the tiered professional development offerings through the Library of Congress. A series of quick reference handouts available online provide self-directed professional development, helping teachers to explore the American Memory collection with titles such as *EyeSpy Math* and *Toolkit for Finding Treasures*. For small to large groups, an excellent array of one hour demonstrations and two hour workshops are available through teleconferences with Library of Congress personnel. These teleconferences are free, and only require that the host site provide paper handouts as well as the necessary hardware to support the teleconference. This is an excellent, low-cost alternative for groups to experience high quality professional development in programs like *Sleuthing with Maps*, *Gathering Community Stories*, and *Make it and Take it!* Finally, for those who wish to attend on-site and hands-on conferences, teachers may attend periodic professional development workshops and summer institutes at the Library of Congress. More information about these conferences is available at the address above or by contacting edoutreach@loc.gov.

- National Archives and Records Administration

  http://www.archives.gov/education/growing-professionally.html

  Like the layered offerings of the Library of Congress above, the National Archives provides professional development in the form of workshops at the school site and at regional and national meetings, through electronic conferences via videoconferencing, and in summer workshops offered in Washington D.C. and at seven regional centers across the nation. Additionally, the National Archives offers two free electronic workshops for students, one exploring the Constitution, and the second an introduction to the archives and the use of primary sources.

- Gilder Lehrman Summer Seminars for Teachers

  http://www.gilderlehrman.org/

  With a focus on high quality history teaching, the week-long Gilder Lehrman Summer Seminars provide intellectual stimulation and collaborative learning with America's premier historians. These well-regarded, tuition-free seminars are held in various sites and include room, board, and a stipend. Past topics include such diverse subjects as *The Colonial Era: Structure and Texture, New York in the Gilded Age*, and *Visions of the American Environment.*

- Organization of American Historians

  http://www.oah.org/

  Committed to building relationships between university and K–12 educators, OAH offers reduced membership fees to precollegiate history teachers. To further teacher learning, OAH grants teachers travel fellowships for their annual meeting, where special sessions are dedicated to the improvement of history teaching and learning. OAH offers professional development at regional conferences as well as their annual meeting.

- Local College or University

  Many universities and colleges maintain speaker's bureaus or lecturers who welcome the opportunity to speak to gatherings of history teachers and students. Additionally, they host lecture series or one-time, guest lectures from distinguished historians.

- State Historical Society programs

  Local, county and state historical societies serve the professional development needs of teachers through guest speakers, special programs related to teaching history, workshops, site visits and other educational services. For example, the Wisconsin Historical Society's Office of School Services recently collaborated with the University of Wisconsin Extension services to offer a full-day workshop, *Engaging the Past through Critical Reading and Inquiry Strategies*, for classroom teachers, grades 4–12.

- Museums, including living history museums

  Local museums provide workshops and lecture series designed for teachers, as well as opportunities to get hands-on experience as a volunteer.

Documents Cited in This Guide

Thinking Like a Historian Chart

Thinking Like a Historian Question Chart

Thinking Like a Historian Instruction and Assessment Planning Rubrics
- **TLH** Historical Process
- **TLH** Historical Categories of Inquiry

Thinking Like a Historian Worksheets
- **TLH** Chart Worksheet
- W-H-W Worksheet
- Website Evaluation Worksheet
- Curriculum Planning for History
- **TLH** Inventory

WHAT QUESTIONS DO WE ASK OF THE PAST? HOW? WHAT? WHERE? WHEN? WHY? WHO?

HOW CAN WE FIND OUT? HOW DO WE EVALUATE THE EVIDENCE?

WHAT MATTERS? WHY DOES IT MATTER?

HOW DO WE KNOW?

HOW DO WE KNOW?

THINKING LIKE A HISTORIAN

CHANGE AND CONTINUITY
- What has changed?
- What has remained the same?

TURNING POINTS
- How did past decisions or actions affect future choices?

THROUGH THEIR EYES
- How did people in the past view their world?

CAUSE AND EFFECT
- What were the causes of past events?
- What were the effects?

USING THE PAST
- How does the past help us make sense of the present?

WHAT QUESTIONS DO WE ASK OF THE PAST? HOW? WHAT? WHERE? WHEN? WHY? WHO?

HOW CAN WE FIND OUT? HOW DO WE EVALUATE THE EVIDENCE?

WHAT MATTERS? WHY DOES IT MATTER?

HOW DO WE KNOW?

HOW DO WE KNOW?

CESA 2, UWW, WHS - 2006

TM

WHAT QUESTIONS DO WE ASK OF THE PAST?
THINKING LIKE A HISTORIAN

CAUSE AND EFFECT	CHANGE AND CONTINUITY	TURNING POINTS	USING THE PAST	THROUGH THEIR EYES
What were the causes of past events?	What has changed? What has remained the same?	How did past decisions or actions affect future choices?	How does the past help us make sense of the present?	How did people in the past view their world?
What were the effects?	• Who has benefited from this change? And why?	• How did decisions or actions narrow or eliminate choices for people?	• How is the past similar to the present?	• How did their worldview affect their choices and actions?
• Who or what made change happen?	• Who has not benefited? And why?	• How did decisions or actions significantly transform people's lives?	• How is the past different from the present?	• What values, skills and forms of knowledge did people need to succeed?
• Who supported change?			• What can we learn from the past?	
• Who did not support change?				
• Which effects were intended?				
• Which effects were accidental?				
• How did events affect people's lives, community, and the world?				

TM

Thinking Like a Historian - Instruction and Assessment Planning Rubric

TLH HISTORICAL PROCESS	Level: 4	Level: 3	Level: 2	Level: 1
Questions Historical events unfolded as different people, groups and institutions with different experiences, needs, ideas and degrees of power interacted • Some questions are better than others. The most interesting and meaningful questions recognize that the past was as complex in the past was as complex as the present. • Historical events unfolded as different people, groups and institutions with different experiences, needs, ideas and degrees of power interacted	• requires attention to multiple perspectives or experiences • requires significant manipulation and use of evidence to support answer • requires analysis that incorporates two or more TLH categories • requires consideration of historical context and change over time	• requires attention to multiple perspectives or experiences • requires some explanation or manipulation of evidence • requires some use of evidence to support answer • may call for compare/ contrast or before/after statements • may not require consideration of historical context	• requires attention to only one perspective or experience • little explanation of evidence required • may not require consideration of historical context	• can be answered with simple yes/no or T/F or fill in the blank • seeks factual responses that require little to no explanation or integration of evidence • does not require consideration of historical context
Evidence Historical sources are not all equal. • It is necessary to consider factors that affect the validity of each source. • Among these are: the creator of the source, the creator's perspective and knowledge about events, the purpose the source was created, and the intended audience • Multiple sources are needed in order to fully understand the complexity and importance of any historical event, era, person, or group. "Dumbing it down" can lead to incorrect, distorted or mythical conclusions.	• uses multiple primary and secondary sources representing a variety of perspectives and/or types of information • identifies author/creator of sources and requires assessment of effect of this on validity and perspective • requires deep analysis of information, motivation and perspectives expressed in sources • requires comparison/contrasts with other sources as part of each source analysis	• uses multiple sources • generally includes combination of primary and secondary sources, although may use one or two of each • identifies author/creator of source, although may not consider the effect of this on validity, perspective or how to evaluate the source(s) • requires some consideration of information, motivation and perspective expressed in source	• uses one or two sources, generally secondary; source(s) presents its account of the past as "authoritative uncontested truth" • no attention to evaluating validity or perspective of the source(s)	• uses one, generally secondary source (textbook, encyclopedia) • no attempt to evaluate validity, perspective or credibility of source
Interpretation Historical interpretations are not all equal. • Some are better than others. • Some are wrong. • Some are misleading.	• analysis and synthesis are fully supported by ideas, concepts and information from multiple sources • explains historical context and reasons for change over time • accounts for multiple perspectives and experiences • makes connections and explains relationships between people, events, ideas, places • explanation of significance is clear and recognizes complex connections between people, events, concepts and/or past and present.	• explains how and why (as well as what, when, where, who) • may concentrate on presenting a linked chronology or juxtaposing two different perspectives • uses some evidence from sources to support explanations • may recognize, but does not analyze reasons for differences, similarities, change over time • offers generalized explanation of significance	• primarily addresses what, when, where, who • responses are low on Bloom's taxonomy (identify and describe) • little use of evidence to support response	• responses are at recall level of Bloom's taxonomy • does not use evidence to support responses

Thinking Like a Historian – Instruction and Assessment Planning Rubric

TLH CATEGORIES OF INQUIRY	Level: 4	Level: 3	Level: 2	Level: 1
Cause & Effect Long term causes and/or effects include: • events, actions or changing patterns of life occurring years or decades before or after the topic of study • existing cultural values or beliefs • political or economic systems that set limits on people's choices	• distinguishes multiple causes and/or multiple effects, including both obvious and intended and more subtle and unintended causes and effects, as well as long and short term causes and effects • recognizes that different groups were affected in different ways	• distinguishes multiple causes of an event &/or multiple effects of an event, including long and short term • recognizes that different groups were affected in different ways	• addresses multiple causes and/or effects • but limited to short term and obvious/intended only	• addresses only one or two causes and/or effects • generally limited to short term and obvious/intended only
Change & Continuity • The past does not repeat itself. • Some aspects of the human experience are constant over long periods of time.	• clearly links change AND continuity to a specific event or series of developments • addresses change and continuity on multiple levels including social, economic, political and/or cultural and over both long and short time periods, trends or patterns • recognizes that different groups were affected in different ways	• clearly links change AND continuity to a specific event or series of developments; • addresses change and continuity in terms of both long and short time periods, trends or patterns • may focus on only one type (social, economic, political or cultural); • recognizes that different groups were affected in different ways	• clearly links change AND continuity to a specific event or series of developments • limited attention to either long OR short time periods and/or focus on only one type (social, economic, political or cultural)	• addresses change OR continuity, failing to address both • connection of change or continuity to the specific event or series of developments not clear
Turning Points New set of parameters or new path of social, political or economic development For example: • end of slavery • rise of waged labor • rise of U.S. as a global power • emergence of Victorian norms of womanhood and manhood	• recognizes both major historical events (wars, industrial revolution) AND less obvious events (migration and demography, social or cultural changes, technological or medical changes) as "turning points" • explains why or how these developments established a new set of parameters or established a different path of historical development	• recognizes major, traditionally-studied historical events as "turning points" (wars, industrial revolution, economic depression) • explains why or how these events established a new set of parameters or established a different path of historical development	• recognizes major, traditionally-studied historical events as "turning points" (wars, industrial revolution, economic depression) • does not explain why or how these events established a new set of parameters or established a different path of historical development	• does not identify any historical changes or event as a "turning point" which set a new course or new set of parameters
Using the Past Historians only use parts of the past. Need to discriminate between which parts of past events are comparable and which are not by considering: • What are the parallels or similarities? • What is different? • All similarities are not "useable" for comparative purposes	• distinguishes elements of, or patterns in, past events or periods that are similar to AND that are different from a contemporary situation • using knowledge of that past event or period draws supportable conclusions about the contemporary situation	• traces developmental relationship, over time and space, between past events or patterns and contemporary events or patterns; • recognizes factors that have contributed to changes over time in the parallel event or pattern	• recognizes similarities and/or differences between past events and contemporary issues, but makes simple, linear connections that jump over decades/centuries of time without addressing impact of intervening developments	• makes no connections between past events or trends and contemporary life
Through Their Eyes • Seek to understand the world view of historical actors and the ways this affected their choices and actions. • Avoid presentism (evaluating the past according to present-day beliefs and actions)	• draws interpretive connections between the ways in which different groups of historical actors understood "their present" (as in level 3) and the ways they responded to the problems, opportunities and choices that confronted them	• recognizes that historical actors brought multiple perspectives to the same event, reflecting differences in class, gender, race/ethnicity, region, religion, age, education, past experiences • does not necessarily connect these perspectives to significant historical developments	• recognizes that people's lives in the past differed in significant way from contemporary, 21st century, life; inc. gender roles, class divisions, personal and national goals, racial/ethnic attitudes, material standards of life • may connect this to personal goals or actions	• uses contemporary values and knowledge [early 21st century] to explain or make sense of past actions or decisions

CHANGE AND CONTINUITY

CAUSE AND EFFECT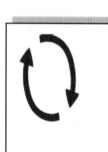

THINKING LIKE A HISTORIAN

TURNING POINTS

USING THE PAST

THROUGH THEIR EYES

™

What – **H**ow – **W**hy Worksheet

Historical Question:

_____
_____?

What do we know?

_____
_____
_____
_____
_____

How do we know?

_____
_____
_____
_____
_____

Why does it matter?

_____
_____
_____
_____
_____

Name _____ Date _____

CESA 2, UWW, WHS - 2007

Worksheet for Evaluating Web Sites

What?	**WHAT is the page/site about? Does it have the kind of information you need?** • Look at the browser title bar, document title, content and links. • Record the title of the web page and web site for citation. Page Title: Website Title:
Who?	**WHO created the page/site? Can you find and verify the author's qualification, whether an individual or organization?** • Look for "About the author/About us" links for author's name and contact information. • Verify author's qualifications in another source, e.g., journal, encyclopedia, directory. • Look for a link to the home page of the Web site where the document lives. • Look at the parts of the URL or address to find organization affiliation. This page/site's author is: Author's qualification:
Where?	**WHERE is the information coming from?** • Look at the address or URL: .edu=educational, .com=commercial, .org=organizational, gov=government, two letter country codes • Look up domain owner with WhoIs search (http://www.networksolutions.com/en_US/whois/index.jhtml) The URL of this page/site is: Type of page/site:

Why?	**WHY is this page/site on the Web and how does it affect the information?**
	• Look at "About us/Mission/Purpose", links, content and advertising.
	• Determine purpose of the site:
	  • Advocacy or "soapbox" (tries to persuade).
	  • Informational (often multiple viewpoints and references).
	  • Business or marketing (tries to sell).
	  • Entertainment.
	• Choose sites whose purposes are compatible with your information needs.
	I believe this page/site is on the web to (circle): advocate/persuade; inform/educate/ sell/business; or entertain. WHY? – Explain:

How?	**HOW accurate or credible is this page/site?** • Examine references and bibliographies. • Verify information in another reputable source (e.g., encyclopedia, journal, book, another Web site-that does not reference or copy this website). • If you notice many errors in spelling, punctuation, grammar, etc., question the accuracy of other information. This page/site (circle one) does / does not have references or a bibliography pointing to the source of information. This page/site (circle one) does / does not have noticeable errors.
When?	**WHEN was the page/site or information created? Is the date important for the timeliness of the content?** • Look for dates. Can you tell what they mean? Publication or copyright date? Last modified or updated? Date any statistics were gathered or published? • Note date you accessed the site. You need this to cite the Web site! I visited (accessed) this page/site on: The date on the page/site is: The date (circle one) does / does not affect the quality or relevance of the content.

Adapted from University of Wisconsin-Madison Libraries Internet Workshop Working Group
The URL of UW-Madison Libraries page is http://www.library.wisc.edu/libraries/instruction/instmat/webeval.htm

CURRICULUM PLANNING FOR HISTORY

COURSE PLAN: Historical Themes — Big Picture

Historically significant developments, types of activities or patterns that students can follow or pick up at multiple times during a school year and as they move from class to class.

The Historical Themes for this Course will be:

UNIT PLAN: Driving Questions

Bridge between historical themes (big picture, above) and key understandings (lesson, below) Promotes deep understanding of historically significant era or events. Focuses on the era or events in terms of historical categories of inquiry. Driving Questions inform lesson design and define what students should know at the end of the unit.

Unit Topic:	Unit Topic:	Unit Topic:	Additional Units...
Driving Question:	Driving Question:	Driving Question:	

LESSON PLAN: Key Understandings — Little Picture

Instructional purpose is determined by the historical themes for the course (big picture) and driving questions for the unit. Explains what students will understand at the end of the lesson. Includes Content, Process and Application.

Key Understandings:	Additional Lessons...	Additional Lessons...
Lesson Content:		
Lesson Process:		
Lesson Application:		

Thinking Like a Historian Inventory

The following components are vital to good history teaching and learning. Read the descriptors as an individual . . . then collaboratively as a team, unit or department. Draw a circle around the number on the scale that in your judgment represents how embedded these attributes are in teaching history in your classroom and school. Be able to defend your ranking with specific examples. If an item is non-existent or ranked low briefly identify in the action step column how it will be included in future curriculum design and instructional delivery. (Please note that on the scale 1 is the lowest and 6 is the highest ranking.)

1. Using driving or essential questions.

    1   2   3   4   5   6   **Comment/Action Step**

2. Explaining how and why historical events may be interpreted differently.

    1   2   3   4   5   6   **Comment/Action Step**

3. Utilizing primary sources as important components in teaching and learning.

    1   2   3   4   5   6   **Comment/Action Step**

4. Developing student assessments tied directly to elements of historical thinking.

    1   2   3   4   5   6   **Comment/Action Step**

5. Understanding bias and how points of view change over time.

    1   2   3   4   5   6   **Comment/Action Step**

6. Teaching to historical imagination and not imagined history.

    1   2   3   4   5   6   **Comment/Action Step**

7. Providing meaningful practical feedback related to content, process and application.

    1   2   3   4   5   6   **Comment/Action Step**

8. Avoiding presentism in examining the past.

    1   2   3   4   5   6   **Comment/Action Step**

9. Extracting meaning from varied sources.

    1   2   3   4   5   6   **Comment/Action Step**

10. Defining what is meant by historical literacy.

    1   2   3   4   5   6   **Comment/Action Step**

11. Applying key concepts and themes such as time, chronology, causality, change, conflict and place in making connections between different eras and events.

    1   2   3   4   5   6   **Comment/Action Step**

12. Interpreting the impact of the past on present-day private and public lives.

    1   2   3   4   5   6   **Comment/Action Step**

13. Crafting meaningful historical questions.

    1   2   3   4   5   6   **Comment/Action Step**

14. Checking the source of sources (credentialing)

    1   2   3   4   5   6   **Comment/Action Step**

15. Formulating conclusions and evaluating these ideas against divergent viewpoints.

    1   2   3   4   5   6   **Comment/Action Step**

16. Reconstructing and reinterpreting the past using new research findings.

    1   2   3   4   5   6   **Comment/Action Step**

17. Developing a sense of historical meaning to see personal place in the stream of time.

    1   2   3   4   5   6   **Comment/Action Step**

18. Analyzing how historians use evidence.

1 2 3 4 5 6

Comment/Action Step

19. Assessing the validity of different interpretations

1 2 3 4 5 6

Comment/Action Step

20. Defending an idea or argument with evidence.

1 2 3 4 5 6

Comment/Action Step

21. Providing opportunities to do something with information that has been learned.

1 2 3 4 5 6

Comment/Action Step

22. Employing skepticism and reasoned judgment.

1 2 3 4 5 6

Comment/Action Step

23. Using quality credentialed websites in historical inquiry.

1 2 3 4 5 6

Comment/Action Step

24. Avoiding gimmicks and "fun" activities that do not promote historical literacy.

1 2 3 4 5 6

Comment/Action Step

25. Providing a balance between depth and coverage in program delivery.

1 2 3 4 5 6

Comment/Action Step

Once completed, come to consensus on the 3 strongest components of history instruction in your classroom or school.

1.

2.

3.

Once completed come to consensus on the 3 weakest components of history instruction that need to be incorporated in what and how you teach in your classroom or school.

1.

2.

3.

Review associated action steps and summarize what you are going to do about it.

Glossary

Many of these terms have discipline-specific meanings that differ from their meanings in common conversation.

agency [historical] refers to people as actively making decisions and engaging in actions that affect their lives and the lives of others; this important concept challenges notions of historical inevitability; the term is most likely to be used in scholarly journals and books.

artifact is any human-made physical object; historians use artifacts as primary sources to understand material culture.

bias slips in when part of the historical evidence is ignored or its importance is discounted without historical justification; it reflects preconceived notion(s) about past events, people or ideas that act as a barrier to investigating all aspects of the event, people or idea.

credentialing [of historical texts] means determining whether the source of information is legitimate and germane to the subject of the historical investigation; credentialing a historical source requires checking the "source of the source."

evidence [historical] is comprised of the primary and secondary sources of information consulted in conducting a historical investigation; [see **primary** and **secondary sources**]

framework [**TLH**] is a conceptual methodology and pedagogical tool for implementing history teaching and learning based on the discipline of historical inquiry and analysis.

historical context refers to the broad developments as well as specific people, events and patterns that preceded, overlapped, and, in some cases, followed the topic of in-depth study; it is not possible to make sense of any historical topic unless we consider it within its historical context.

historical record is the totality of the historical sources, primary and secondary, that are reasonably available and/or examined in the course of research.

historical imagination is the art (and science) of being able to use the tools of **historical literacy** to interpret the events of the past; it recognizes and respects the difference between past and present

historical literacy is the acquisition of a set of inquiry and analytical skills that allow a person to conduct a sound historical investigation and draw supportable conclusions; it is the active combination of the historical process and historical categories of inquiry

historiography is the study or explanation of changes over time in the ways that historians have interpreted a past event or era; interpretations of past events or eras change over time because the questions we ask about the past change, new historical sources become available and/or historical sources are analyzed in new ways.

hook is a lesson openers designed to engage students' interest in a historical topic

imagined history is the presentation or assignment that gives a false picture or oversimplification of the past; it collapses past and present into an undifferentiated world

interpretation [historical] is the analysis and synthesis of a past event(s), people or ideas supported by legitimate research and use of primary and secondary sources

presentism means to use values, worldviews, beliefs, ethics, hopes and fears of the present day to judge, hypothesize or draw conclusions about how people felt, thought, acted or should have acted in the past

primary sources are sources created at the time an event occurred or by people who were there when the event occurred; these include letters, public speeches, newspaper articles, census reports, court records, private diaries, photographs, songs, e-mail messages, birth records, legislative debates and oral accounts.

pseudo-history is writing or interpretation about the past that is based on inadequate or illegitimate sources or incomplete analysis

secondary sources are interpretive accounts made after the historical event has passed. Authors of secondary sources rely on primary sources and other secondary sources for their information about the event; these include journal or magazine articles, books, textbooks, maps, movies, documentaries, museum exhibits and living history re-enactments.

time and space [historical] "time" refers to the passage of chronological time, as measured by days, months, years, centuries, millennia; "space" means geographical place, as defined by village, city, countryside, region, nation, empire.

NOTES

NOTES

NOTES

NOTES

NOTES